CRAZY

A MEMOIR

BY
H. R. STOKES III

Copyright © 2012 by H. R. Stokes III
All rights reserved.

Library of Congress Catalogue Card Number:
Pending

ISBN-13: 978-1469925189
ISBN-10: 1469925184

All lyrics by Lowell George printed by permission of Elizabeth George.

On Your Way Down
Words and Music by Allen Toussaint
© 1972 (Renewed 1999) SCREEN GEMS-EMI MUSIC INC. and WARNER-TAMERLANE PUBLISHING CORP.
All Rights Reserved International Copyrights Secured Used by Permission *Reprinted by Permission of Hal Leonard and Alfred Music Publishing Co., Inc.*

Disclaimer: This is a memoir and the stories within are real. I lived them all. However, parenthetically speaking, I was often fucked up during the times described, and therefore may have understated a little in the writing of this book. Some of the names are real while others are real fake. I did that for fun and to protect those that are ashamed of their pasts. You know who you are, posers. The dialogue is as I remember. However, after thirty to forty years, the memory fails somewhat, and I had to take artistic license. Nevertheless, this is a true recollection of the facts as I recall them. Please note: I reduced the number of vulgarities I typically use for the benefit of the reader. However, if you would like to contact me, I would be more than happy to recite any of the missing expletives you can stomach.

WARNING!

If you don't like sex, drugs, and rock 'n' roll
or the word "motherfucker,"
enter at your own risk,
preferably drunk.

*To Lowell George and all
my friends who walk these pages*

ACKNOWLEDGEMENTS

I would like to thank Michelle Huels,
my muse, my masterful editor.
Without her inspiration and dedicated persistence,
this book would not have been written.

Cover photo: Michelle Huels

ACCOMPLICES

I would also like to thank Shellie,
Tom, Tommie Lou, Lonni,
Austin the Magnificent, Jill the Pencil Point,
"Sista" Lee, and our complicit mastermind
Danielle. Without their invaluable time,
feedback, and encouragement, this crime
might not have been committed.

Now please join me in a moment of
silence in recognition of the
awesome Createspace publishing
team that drove the getaway car all
the way to you, the reader.

We are each in our own way responsible, emotionally available, hard working, fathers, sons, husbands, and generous human beings who have been a collection and assortment, at one time or another, of elitists, heads, charlatans, outlaws, hot rodders, dharma bums, mavericks, truth seekers, cowboys, social lepers, surfers, commune dwellers, anarchists, bohemians, usual suspects, unnamed sources, wayfaring strangers, gamblers, angel-headed hipsters, beatniks, poachers, bikers, dreamers, adventurers, lunatics, explorers, wordsmiths, pundits, rebels, dervishes, visionaries, mental patients, droogs, rakes, reprobates, mysterious strangers, seers, individualists, dissenters, rip-offs, independents, poets, artists, entrepreneurs, mercenaries, pirates, dealers, smugglers, imagineers, creators, hustlers, rastas, pariahs, derelicts, freaks, convicts, hippies, social climbers, status quo worshippers, drug fiends, and drunkards; yet, most of all .....survivors.

...Louis Romano, 2004

PROLOGUE

Now I smuggled some smokes and folks from Mexico
Baked by the sun, every time I go to Mexico, and I'm still
And I've been kicked by the wind, robbed by the sleet
Had my head stoved in and I'm still on my
feet and I'm willin', oh I'm willin

... "Willin'" by Lowell George

I turned sixty today. My reign in the world of international drug smuggling has been over for some time. I had every intention of writing this story before my sixtieth birthday, but I couldn't quite seem to make the cutoff. Life on the edge of intrigue and danger has slowed down considerably, but man, what a great run it was.

The hippie movement of the sixties had a huge impact on me, maybe more than for most. I was one of those white college boys who figured out there was a ton of money to be made in the weed business. "Sex, drugs, and rock 'n' roll" was our mantra, the peace sign our badge of courage. I thought of myself as kind of a folk hero during that time, at least a legend in my own mind. There were many of us who were convinced we were the titans of a new industry; the next Phillip Morris, you could say.

This was way before the War on Drugs became a cliché or was even part of the vernacular, and when the DEA was just a twinkle in the eye of a bureaucrat's wet dream. It was a time when Richard Nixon formed a commission to decide whether or not marijuana should be legalized. It was a time when "the times they are a changin'." I was convinced weed was the future. "Not so fast cowboy!" the Man shouted. Turns out, the commission our beloved Nixon formed to research legalization simply morphed into the DEA, and they, of course, soon became my biggest nemesis. "Game on, motherfuckers!"

CHAPTER ONE

Whoa I am just a vagabond, a drifter on the run
And eloquent profanity, it rolls right off my tongue

... *"Roll Um Easy" by Lowell George*

I was born Harry Russell Stokes III. My older sister Lee wanted to name the newly arriving baby Sandy. Therefore, I was called Sandy even before I was born and have been known as Sandy my whole life. The only time I was called Harry was on the first day of school each year when the teacher was taking roll call and making seat assignments—well, maybe also, during a routine traffic stop…or when being read my rights. So the name Harry always had a slight edge to me. However, as I grew into a man, I began to like the name. It sounded strong, Harry Russell Stokes III. It just never rang true to who I was. I was Sandy.

I grew up in San Antonio, Texas, in the township of Terrell Hills, an affluent neighborhood inside the city limits. We had our own police force to "serve and protect"; however, there was little crime and little for them to do. From my perspective, it seemed they only focused on harassing the Mexican laborers that were there primarily to keep our neighborhood pristine. Terrell Hills had its own ZIP code as well: 78209. Some called themselves "09ers" because they assumed there was a plus sign added to their social status if lucky enough to reside there. Every large city has one: a Beverly Hills, a Brentwood, an Oak Park, and of course, our own little Terrell Hills. We lived on Arcadia Place, a street of block parties, a neighborhood band called the Arcadia Cats, shared family vacations to the coast, and cocktail hours, endless cocktail hours.

Regardless, it was a great place to grow up. All the streets were shaded with beautiful live oaks ideal for climbing and hiding. There were also plenty of mesquite trees with long protruding thorns that would stab the bottoms of your bare feet if you weren't careful. The homes seemed like mansions from my four-foot-tall vantage point, and many of them really were. Some were especially impressive, with gated entrances and acres of well-manicured lawns. We were never intimidated by the security of these places and snuck into all of them to play. Nothing was off limits to us.

Alf was my best friend while growing up on Arcadia Place. He and another friend Mike and I would ride our bikes and play all day, seldom checking in with our parents. My bike had a siren that was loud as hell and difficult to distinguish from a squad car, especially at high speeds. I would go screaming down the hill past my house as I hauled ass toward Alf's. I made damn sure the playing cards that were clothes-pinned to the bike frame and rumbling in the spokes were fresh and firm, making it roar like a motorcycle. The only thing missing was a set of flashing lights. However, I never took on the role of a cop; my goal was simply to terrorize the neighborhood.

I must say, for a small tike I had a hell of a temper. Alf always outweighed me by fifty pounds and was maybe as much as two feet taller. He was a big ol' boy, but I could chase that motherfucker around the neighborhood if my temper flared, and he was sure to stay at least twenty feet ahead. One day, I thought he had broken a toy rifle of mine, and by god, there was hell to pay. I chased him down our street and around his house until he locked himself inside. He kept peering out the window at me while I ranted and raved, too scared to come back out. There was no messin' with me once I went off.

The long summer days and nights of South Texas offered plenty of freedom to move around unsupervised, sometimes finding trouble as we traveled miles and miles around the neighborhood. I played lots of Cowboys and Indians with Alf and Mike and all the other kids on our block. I threw rocks, had a BB gun and killed a few birds, maybe broke a few windows, and even got kicked out of Sunday school; but choosing the life of an international drug smuggler? It never occurred to me I'd actually end up being a real outlaw.

Things were good for me in Terrell Hills. I used to walk home from Cambridge Elementary School kicking an empty beer can and trying to knock it as noisily as possible down the street for blocks and blocks, attempting to make it all the way home. Other times, I would smash two empty cans onto the heels of my tennis shoes and "clang, clang, clang, clang" down the street. Sometimes I would stop at the "Ize Box" to buy a Fudgsicle or a Slow Poke. It was one of the first convenience stores in our neighborhood and still sold block ice. This was the same place where I constantly went with my dad to buy that ice for the unlimited liquor consumed on our family trips to Port Aransas or Nuevo Laredo, Mexico, not to mention at home. Those motherfuckers knew how to drink, just not how to stop.

This was the late fifties, the time of black-and-white TV, cold metal TV trays, and those disgusting metallic-tasting Salisbury steak and mashed potatoes frozen TV dinners. Oh my god, how I loved them. Admittedly, I spent many hours fixated on our small black-and-white TV screen. As with most kids, I loved cartoons. One afternoon, I saw a *Yogi and Boo-Boo* episode on TV. Yogi had wrapped and tied his arms with leaved branches and after waving them up and down, took off flying. I was convinced I could do the same. Hell, I saw him do it!

A few weeks later, my father was out in the front yard trimming our hedges. Coincidentally, the same kind of branches I had seen in the cartoon were tossed all over our front lawn. "No way," I thought to myself, realizing this was my chance to prove my theory. I grabbed my Confederate cap and my sister's steel skates and proceeded outside to rally my dad for my project under development. I asked him to wrap and tie the fresh cut branches to my extended arm, and he was happy to oblige.

With branches attached, I readied myself for flight. I stood on the sidewalk in front of my house flapping and flapping, and then started to roll forward to gain speed. I kept my head down, cap in place, skates strapped on, and took off down the hill. I was confident! I flapped and flapped and flapped...nothing. I went back for another try. I forget how many attempts it took me to come to the realization it wasn't going to work. "What have I missed?" I asked myself, trying to size things up. Oh man, I just knew I could do it—and eventually did. Optimism was always my ally.

I identified with all the heroes of the Saturday morning lineup and loved reinventing myself with each character: Davy Crockett, the Lone Ranger and Tonto, Zorro, Robin Hood, and

Sky King. Saturday mornings, *Davy Crockett* came on first. I would watch with intensity, wearing my own replicated coonskin cap. Once *Davy Crockett* was over, I would run up the stairs to my bedroom to change into my Zorro costume, then, back downstairs to the den for a thirty-minute stint of *Zorro*. I was captivated. At the end of the *Zorro* episode, it was back upstairs to exchange my cape and mask for my Robin Hood ensemble, complete with bow and arrow, but sporting the same Zorro mask. I lived and breathed those characters and have enjoyed changing identities as needed ever since.

I maintained my affinity with Robin Hood and Zorro throughout my smuggling career. I thought their purpose and ideals were similar to mine, and I was certain I was following in their footsteps. After all, I was an outlaw marauding in the forest with my band of merry men. Ironically, my sister informed me that my grandmother Mamo had once said to her, "You know, Sandy really is a good boy, he's just got a little criminal in him." I have always felt that was mighty understanding of my conservative grandmother. I wasn't a criminal, however. I was just an outlaw.

Once, I built a raft in my garage from scraps of wood and nailed it all together with probably more than a thousand nails. I loved slamming those nails into the wood. I wanted to be Huckleberry Finn and float it down the Mississippi while waving good-bye to my parents. Adventure was my middle name! Instead, my dad was kind enough to rope it to the roof of our station wagon and take Alf, Mike, and me down to Port Aransas for its maiden voyage. It worked, thanks to the large truck inner tubes I had filled with air and fastened to the bottom. There Alf, Mike, and I were floating down a canal in Port Aransas with our homemade oars, reeling in our success—the first of many maritime adventures.

When I was about ten, I was playing with some kids at the neighbor's house up the street, when a few of us decided it was time to run away from home and ride freight trains, just as the hobos had done in all the black-and-white movies we'd seen. It was harmless enough; none of us were mad at our parents. We were just looking for the excitement of riding the trains on our own—every boy's dream. Three of us laid out our plans to run away: Mike, Russ, and I.

That night, as my parents and sister were readying themselves for bed, I was readying myself for my new life on the lam. I packed a kerchief and grabbed my walking stick, just as I had seen the hobos do before me. I scribbled a note on my Big Chief tablet that read only one word: "Farewell!" I quietly slipped down the staircase and out the front door. It was about ten at night, way past dark. I was beyond excited and stopped at Mike's house first, just a few doors down. I stood below his second story bedroom window and began to toss rocks against the pane. After what seemed like forever, he finally raised the sash and looked down at me in his side yard. I quietly hollered up to him while waving my hands, "Let's go!" Mike leaned out his window and whispered back to me, "I can't, I just took a bath." "What?" I responded, and Mike repeated, "I can't, I just took a bath." I shook my head in disbelief, and murmured back, "OK—I guess."

It was now time to move on to Russ's house. I decided I would just have to go it alone until I got there. I wasn't afraid yet. I had never walked to Russ's house alone or at night. My mother had driven me over there the few times I had visited. As you might guess, I never could find it.

Puzzled about my options, I decided I would head to my grandmother's house instead. It was around midnight by then, and I was starting to get a little worried. However, I was still committed and determined. I was about five miles into my journey, crossing the Olmos Park Dam, when an older couple pulled up in their car and yelled out, "Hey, kid! What are you doing out here? Are you in trouble?" I simply replied, "I'm going to my grandma's." Thank goodness those were more innocuous times, as this couple gave me a ride to her house. My parents had alerted my grandmother that I was missing, and she found the fact that I had now shown up at her house quite comical. She was one hell of a grandmother and seemed to understand my need to wander.

By junior high, I had become friends with a kid named Stevie. He was an extremely influential character. I can almost say he had a spell on me. Stevie was a kid ahead of his time. He was aware of all the hip things coming out of California and was wealthy, so could afford the best of everything. He had the trendiest clothes, the most advanced stereo system, and the biggest album collection, including all the most recent releases. Stevie was as clever as he was funny, but also the cockiest, most defiant motherfucker I'd ever met. I loved that about him.

I met Stevie in homeroom. Madras print shirts had come into fashion that year and my mother had bought me a knock-off. I was so proud of that shirt I wore it almost every day for weeks in a row. One day in homeroom Stevie asked, "Do you ever plan on changing that shirt?" I didn't know him at the time and, therefore, was completely devastated by his comment. I don't believe I ever wore that shirt again; however, we became best friends after this exchange.

These were difficult years for kids our age because status suddenly became important. Stevie and I handled it the same way. We were both incorrigible and encouraged each other in that direction. We never made a move without checking with each other first. The hippie movement was beginning to surface and both of us were very susceptible to its rising influence. There were many others besides me who found Stevie just as alluring, but unfortunately, most of them are now dead due to drug overdoses. Stevie's personal influence was astounding.

Stevie and I had both gotten our drivers licenses at age fourteen. By age fifteen, my license had already been suspended due to numerous tickets. One day a cute little freshman from Alamo Heights High named Cynthia picked me up in her father's Oldsmobile 442. I couldn't wait to get behind the wheel of this badass machine. It had four on the floor and was a convertible. This was a true muscle car. I persuaded her to let me drive. That was a bad decision on her part, but she was young and I'm sure I was rather convincing. "It'll be OK" always seemed to reassure the girls.

We drove down Austin Highway to the Frontier Drive-in, a popular hangout spot for all the Northside kids. It was Sunday after church, and I was still dressed in tie and jacket. After arriving at the Frontier, we made our loop around the parking lot as was customary. Then I pulled back onto Austin Highway, gunning the engine and spinning the tires. Before I knew it, there were flashing police lights behind me. I took a right on Vandiver and pulled over. Since my license had already been suspended, I was sure I was screwed.

As the cop got out of his car and headed toward us on foot, I looked at Cynthia and said, "Hold on!" I threw that 442 into first gear and took off! I saw the cop in my rearview mirror charging back to his car, and the chase was on. I hauled ass around the streets ahead of me as fast as that 442 could go. I was squealing through the neighborhood, slamming that car from gear to gear.

It was a noisy, fucking chase, eventually involving eight cop cars following behind me in hot pursuit. The whole time Cynthia kept her face hidden in her hand with her elbow leaning on the armrest. Occasionally, she would plead, "Sandy, please stop!" I would respond between power shifts, "I can't right now, but I will soon, promise!" With all the lights flashing and sirens screaming, some of the neighbors came outside their homes and stood in their yards, witnessing this incredible chase. This car was fast, faster than the police cars of that period, and I finally lost them all!

I knew a girl in an adjacent neighborhood, so I headed in that direction. The garage door was open, so I whipped in and quickly lowered it. I pounded on their back screen door and when they responded, there we stood trembling in fear. "I've got some hoodlums chasing me," I said. "Could we please hide out here for a moment?" I was dressed in my Sunday best and at fifteen looked pretty goddamned wholesome. Her mother responded cautiously, "Well, I guess so, young man."

Cops were still zooming around the neighborhood and continually passing in front of her house. The mom was bewildered and asked, "What do you think is going on?" I responded in all seriousness, "There were some bad guys that were chasing us and I'm sure they're looking for them." It was the best I could come up with in my desperate state.

All of a sudden there was a knock on the door. Yep, the cops had seen smoke billowing from the car and apparently pouring out of the vented garage door. Busted! But in my defense, I had outrun all eight of those motherfuckers. I was goddamned proud! The mom answered the door and, as expected, a policeman was standing there. He asked the mom, "Do you happen to own a white Oldsmobile 442?" She responded, "No," and slowly turned toward me, motioning me to come to the door; "But I think this young man may be able to help you." "Ouwee, I'm in trouble now!" I said to myself.

I went outside to find an entire police force parked in front of the house and tried to look innocent, even though my actions said otherwise. Another policeman approached me and said in a slow drawl, "Boy, I was about to fill your ass full of buckshot had it not been for that little lady with you," then spit a wad of tobacco in emphasis. He was a big ol' boy. I don't believe I had anything to say back, so I just nodded. I ended up receiving eight tickets: seven stop sign violations and one for driving without a license, but incredibly, not one speeding ticket. Cynthia's parents were pretty upset with me, but I never heard a word from them.

Sometime during 1967, my dad had bought my mom a new Mustang convertible. It was royal blue with a light-blue convertible top. Man, I thought this was one of the coolest cars ever. Unfortunately, I had already destroyed the 1965 white Mustang my mother had previously owned. The problem was that I had never thought of them as her cars in the first place. I always considered them mine. My father once informed me after returning from the transmission repair center, "Sandy, the mechanic has never seen a transmission as destroyed as the one in the white Mustang." Damn, that was pretty strong. "Never?" I questioned with pride. "No never!" he snapped. I had just been learning to drive, and drive fast was how I liked to roll. So of course, I had to see what that baby could take.

As a result, the new blue Mustang was off limits to me; well, at least while my parents were awake. I used to push it quietly out of the driveway after midnight and joyride in "my" new convertible for hours on end. I was careful not to be as hard on the transmission of my new car as I had been on the previous one. I'm afraid the tires were a different story. They paid the price of a new teenage driver.

Later that year, one cold December night, I snuck my friend Frannie from her house. She was a sweet little girl who I secretly adored. I had met her at Amery Oliver's dance studio. We were both learning the proper dances such as the waltz, foxtrot, swing, and rumba; all the ones our parents thought we should know for the upcoming cotillions. "Really, wouldn't the alligator be sufficient?" I protested in my head while gliding around the dance floor with Frannie.

That night it was raining, and raining hard. Frannie and I were speeding around Loop 410 at seventy miles per hour. I assumed everything was cool. The Mustang, however, seemed to have a different idea. It started to hydroplane and after the slightest little movement began to fishtail. First, the rear end went to the left, then back to the right; and before we knew it, we were spinning round and round, out of control, going seventy miles per hour down the highway. Oh, my god, we did close to three complete loops before spinning and sliding onto the grass meridian, where we spun around again, and then into the oncoming traffic on the opposite side of the highway, still maintaining a high rate of speed. From my rearview mirror, I could see cars swerving to try to miss us. I had never been so terrified.

Then I heard a little girl screaming, "We are going to be killed, we are going to be killed!" However, when I looked over, I found Frannie sitting stone-faced and frozen in fear. She hadn't said a word. I realized it must've been me I heard screaming, not Frannie.

I was fucking white with terror when the Mustang slid back onto the grass meridian and stopped. We looked at each other in total disbelief with our hearts pounding, stunned there wasn't a scratch on us. No fucking way! How we had survived this incredible series of twists and turns was beyond comprehension. I meekly got us back on the highway and headed directly to Frannie's to drop her off and head back home. I don't believe

Frannie ever snuck out with me again. Who could blame her? This was just the beginning of the many dangerous times I would thwart death and live to tell the story. Seems I continually thought of myself as invincible, possibly immortal. Crazy.

As I grew older, there were lots of distractions: football games, debutante parties, dances at the Mule Stall dance hall at Alamo Heights High School, and the annual festival, "Night In Old San Antonio." There was also falling in love with my high school girlfriend Lynda, and then remembering when the skanky bitch dumped me! I was young and unsure of myself, and after a year and a half of constant make-out sessions, I can only assume she wanted to have sex. I was way too immature to know how to broach that subject. She dumped me for someone that could. I was heartbroken.

After our breakup, I felt like an outsider and gravitated toward a more accepting crowd. I smoked my first joint at sixteen years old. This was months before the rest of my friends began their experimentation. I turned Stevie, Gary, Jamie, and Bob on to my new discovery. We immediately became potheads! It wasn't long before we were sticking anything and everything in our mouths and even in our veins. We were eating black mollies, whites, Valium, Quaaludes, multiple barbiturates including reds, yellow jackets, and blues, and also LSD and magic mushrooms. Heroin became commonplace as well. For us, smack was just a weekend folly. Dangerous, hell yes, but it was everywhere. Terrell Hills was rampant with the shit, involving girls and boys alike. At least fifty of us were all shooting up, everybody as far as I could tell.

San Antonio was a huge depot for this drug, as near to the border as we were. During these times, Fred Gomez Carrasco was a legend and supplied the entire country with black tar heroin from the extremely Mexican south side of San Antonio. He was eventually gunned down in a televised escape from Huntsville State Prison. Many innocent people were killed during his brazen attempt. As sickening as our involvement now seems, it was exciting and commonplace then. The hippie movement was upon us. The drug culture ruled! We smoked weed and took as much LSD as we could get our hands on and then took heroin to come down. Yeah, baby; regretfully it was nothing but a party, at least for us.

My mother once grabbed my arms and stood me in front of the mirror, frantically asking, "What the hell have you taken?" With my eyes red and dilated, and ripped on LSD, I responded with my usual indifference, "Nothing." The very next day, she confronted me again at the breakfast table and said, "I used to think these friends of yours were a bad influence on you. However, now I realize you're the bad influence!" She was probably right.

Night after night, I secretly pushed my mother's Mustang out of the drive by hand and let it roll down the hill of Arcadia Place. Then after a short distance, I fired it up and headed off into the night to get Stevie. We would speed down Broadway to The Sunken Gardens in Brackenridge Park for a rendezvous with hundreds of other teens out doing the same. It was nothing for us to drop acid and stroll through the gardens for hours, tripping our brains out. It was a blast! As I recall, Stevie and I dropped acid together close to one hundred times in 1968. We were sixteen years old and totally out of control!

Stevie and I had really gotten into experimenting with drugs by this time. One night we took some Marazine and NoDoz, a hallucinogenic combination. Marazine is a seasickness pill derived from the drug Belladonna. Belladonna is renowned for its hallucinogenic properties. Neither one of us had any of this data beforehand, primarily because we were sixteen years old. We had only heard that you could get fucked up on it. So we took it. Apparently, we took too much. The effects left us, literally, out of our minds. We ended up somewhere in south San Antonio in a dangerous part of town. How we got there is still a complete mystery to me. However, there we were, driving around in my first car, a pale green Chevy Corvair, as we had heard there was a party at some house. We were clueless where it was, but were looking for it anyway. We parked the Corvair and walked around the neighborhood, peeking in windows to see if we recognized any of our friends or spotted any activity.

Eventually, after looking into some family's window, we went to their door and knocked. We were out of our minds by then. Some man came storming out his front door and in a fit of rage asked us, "What the fuck do you kids want?" "We're looking for the party," we replied, as if that was going to satisfy this irate homeowner. He told us, "Get the fuck off my property, and now!" We proceeded to stumble down the steps and "got the fuck out of there," apologizing in our retreat as best we could.

Well, this drug we had taken had very strange effects. It produced what I would call absolute and utter psychosis. We meandered down his sidewalk and got into either his truck or somebody else's, thinking it was my Corvair. That's how crazy this shit was. We were sitting in that truck when the police showed up. They appeared at the window and asked me, "Is this your truck?" I, of course, thought it was. Hell, we both thought it was! I said back to the officer, "Yes, sir." He asked me to produce my keys and start it for him. As I was trying to get my keys into the ignition, I suddenly became aware of reality and said, "Oh, this isn't my car. There it is in front of us." Oh shit, both Stevie and I realized our error at the same moment and then immediately returned to our delusional state of mind.

Apparently, we were so fucked up that once we got into my car, the police had difficulty getting us out in order to make an arrest. Therefore, one of the officers got in with us and drove us to the station. I remember shouting at him from the backseat, "You're grinding the gears goddamn it, stop it!" How I got to the backseat is still in question. The police later told my dad they normally took perpetrators to police headquarters in a squad car, but said, "these boys were so out of their minds, we thought it best just to take theirs." Now that's fucked up!

Stevie and I were taken to the juvenile holding center at police headquarters. It was a big room with fluorescent lights, resembling a classroom with school chairs and attached desks, much like in high school. Stevie and I were sitting around in our clueless state, all the while bringing our empty fingers to our mouths and taking long, deliberate drags, as if we were actually smoking. From time to time, we'd become aware there were no cigarettes, and assuming we'd dropped them, would get on our hands and knees and begin frantically searching. I can only imagine what the cops must have been thinking. Apparently, we represented a completely new breed and only a small sample of what they were to encounter in the coming years.

Unfortunately, that was not the end of it. We were both in and out of our drug-induced psychosis at the police station when my father arrived to take me home. I don't know what the police told him, but I'm sure it wasn't anything good. Things were about to get interesting. We were driving home in his Buick Regal, and as we approached Arcadia, I saw some kids playing in the street. It was three in the fucking morning! As my dad approached the kids, it appeared to me that he was going to hit one, and I started freaking out! I slammed my palms on the dash of his car and screamed, "You're going to hit him, you're going to hit him!" and, damn, from my whacked out vision, my dad actually hit him! I was mortified as I turned and peered through the back window, expectantly looking for the carnage... but there was nothing. Oh my god, my awareness had resumed momentarily. I looked at him, and he looked at me and said, "Son, I just need to get you home." Man, what the fuck could he have been thinking? I, on the other hand, casually moved back into my psychotic state. I was cool, sure hoped he was.

When we arrived home, my dad wanted me to sleep in his bedroom. My mother happened to be out of town, leaving her bed available. (My parents slept in twin beds, which I hoped was common at that time.) I was happy to oblige and tucked myself right in and went to sleep. It was now close to three thirty in the morning, and I can only guess how extremely whooped my dad was from the crisis he had just endured. However, I was still jacked up on the dozen NoDoz combo I had taken earlier and awoke a couple of hours later. I decided I would get dressed and take my mother's Mustang down to the dealership for some repairs I thought were necessary.

I spoke to my mother in the kitchen before I left to let her know where I was going. All was well as far as I was concerned. I arrived at the dealership and proudly telephoned my dad to let him know what I was busy doing. He groggily answered the phone, "Hello?" "Hey dad, it's Sandy. I just wanted to let you know I am down at the dealership with the Mustang getting it repaired." "What? Where the hell are you?" he demanded. "Down at the dealership," I said. "I talked to Mom in the kitchen and let her know what I was going to do. Is everything cool?" My dad, freaking out by now, couldn't believe what he was hearing and screamed back, "Your mom is out of town! Get your ass back here now!" I was as shocked as he was at this news, thinking I'd seen my mom. "Be right there dad," I cheerfully responded. I really don't remember much more than that, but I can only imagine how utterly perplexed and confused my dad must have been. I never took Marazine again, but that was not the end of the shit my father had to tolerate. I was sixteen years old, and unfortunately, only at the beginning of my drug involvement.

There was a strange dichotomy in my high school experience. Despite my rampant drug use, I played football, ran track, and was on the swim and dive team. In addition, I was voted "Best Dancer," with my picture published in the high school yearbook. Sometime during my junior year, the swim coach called me to the side of the pool during practice and confronted me: "Sandy, I understand that you are smoking and drinking?" I, in turn, said, "Well, there is some truth to that, but the whole team smokes and drinks. Is there a problem?" "Oh really?" Coach Masser responded, "You're saying that everybody on the team smokes and drinks?" I answered casually, "Yeah, what seems to be the big deal?"

Coach Masser then blew his whistle and brought practice to a halt. He lined everybody up in single file, poolside, and one by one, confronted each member of the team with me at his side: "Sandy claims that you smoke and drink." Well, imagine how I felt about all this, as one by one each member of the team said, "No way. Of course not, Coach!" I was released from the swim team at the end of the proceedings.

As I was doing my research for this book, I thumbed through my 1968 Olmos yearbook and came upon a dedication to me from Derrick Silvey, the All State Champion Swimmer. It read, "Hey Sandy, you big stud you, sure did miss you the on the swim team this year! Fuck Coach! Best regards, Derrick." I regret to say Derrick is now dead from a drug overdose. Unfortunately, four of the six in my tight high school gang are also dead from drug overdoses: Stevie, Gary, Doug, and Jamie. Bob and I are the only ones left, and miraculously, he is a practicing attorney in Houston, Texas.

During my senior year, I had saved up enough money from mowing lawns and washing cars to buy a Volkswagen van. I bought it from a friend named Mark. It was a hippie van; I had never been so excited! This van looked atrocious, but I was thrilled with it. The color was primer-gray, and an old primer-gray, at that. I don't believe it came with any back seats, but I would've taken them out anyway. I set up a foam pad complete with Mexican blanket in the rear of the vehicle to act as a bed. I hung a Chinese lantern in the center, dangling from the headliner. It was 1969, the beginning of the hippie movement, as far as Terrell Hills was concerned. My van screamed "hippie" and I couldn't have been more proud.

As I drove around the streets of San Antonio, this ugly van drew lots of attention, negative attention. As a rebel teen, who didn't love that? My father absolutely hated this van parked in front of his beautiful house in our upscale neighborhood. It was horrific for him. He hated it so much that he offered to buy me another—one that didn't look so bad. Well, hell, I was in favor of that! However, shortly before I was to rid the neighborhood of my primer-gray eyesore, I needed to take it one step further. I took a can of spray paint and in large, bold letters wrote on each side, "Don't laugh, your daughter may be inside." I raised more than eyebrows with that one. My sister always claimed I liked a lot of shock value. I seemed to embrace anarchy. Much like the night of my high school graduation when I took a handful of LSD for the graduation ceremony. I was completely out of my mind as I walked across the stage to receive my diploma that night. Ah, high school, just happy to have survived. Thankfully, I graduated from Alamo Heights High School, class of '69. I can remember thinking how lucky I was to be graduating that year, '69 having other connotations. At seventeen years of age, I found that to be an incredibly fortunate coincidence. Class of '69—how could I be so lucky?

I attended San Antonio College that fall and tooled around town in my new used burnt-orange Volkswagen van my dad had purchased to replace my primer-gray. I decked it out much like the previous van. I painted American flags on the two concave windows in the rear. I removed the bench seats from the back and placed the same foam pad and Mexican blanket on top of the interior back platform. I hung the Chinese lantern again from the headliner. I had a bamboo-beaded curtain from Pier One that hung as a divider between the front seat and rear compartments. There were two canvas folding chairs that acted as rear seats. This time, though, I added a four-foot tall hookah pipe with multiple hoses that sat in the corner behind the driver's seat. It was my own little mobile apartment. It was my motherfucking "Magic Bus."

This van, in full dress, screamed at the police, "I smoke marijuana and take LSD." I might as well have thrown rocks at them. I was pulled over constantly. Additionally, my long, blond hair and Indian garb seemed to incite "the fucking Pigs," as we used to call them. It wasn't long before my friend Allen and I were stopped in my smoke-filled van and promptly arrested for possession of marijuana and narcotics paraphernalia. We were both only seventeen years old.

Allen and I were in pretty big trouble and both our parents were extremely angry. My father came to me one day and said, "Sandy, would you be willing to enlist in the Army in order to have this arrest negated and all charges dropped?" This was one of the few times I can remember my father "asking" me if I would do something rather than "telling" me what to do. I disdained authority and all authoritative figures. From my teenage perspective my father fell headfirst into that category. However, his request had been presented so sincerely, I couldn't help but agree. United States Army, here I come.

CHAPTER TWO

It's a crass and raucous crackass place
It's a plague upon the human race
It's a terrible illness, it's a terrible case
And usually permanent when it takes place

… "Teenage Nervous Breakdown" by Lowell George

I volunteered for the draft in early 1970 at eighteen years of age. Volunteering for the draft kept my enlistment term to the shortest time possible. Two years was all I would have to do. The Vietnam War was at its height, and the news reflected many casualties among our troops. I was scared to death. I was a hippie. Peace and love were my beliefs. The war went totally against my grain. Though I had agreed to go, I needed to try to keep myself safe and out of Vietnam.

I was first stationed at Fort Lewis, Washington, for basic training. I had come up with what I thought was some clever shit. I had figured out that if I stayed in basic training for an extended length of time, my enlistment period might be up before I was sent to Vietnam. My goal was simple: stay alive, regardless of the consequences. I was a tie-dyed hippie in Army greens. There was no way I was going to Vietnam! Although basic training was only a nine-week course, I turned it into nine months, taking it three separate times. Toward the middle or the end of each session, I would head over to the infirmary claiming to be sick. They would stick a thermometer in my mouth, and once the nurse would turn her head, I would take it out and rub it furiously on my pant leg. The friction would raise the temperature of the thermometer to a very sickly 102 to 103 degrees. I was immediately admitted into the hospital. I would use the same procedure to stay a minimum of four days, because if you missed that amount, you had to start basic training over from the beginning. This meant a transfer to a new company, new barracks, and new everything. You could really rack up some time with that shit.

Additionally, during my second stint in basic training, I tried to pull off a bad back routine. I first went to the library and studied up on what serious illness I could acquire that would not be detectable as fraud. I found it: back pain. Upon my arrival at the new student company, I jumped out of the truck with my duffel bag and immediately folded over in extreme pretend pain. "Here I go," I said to myself. I spent the next few weeks bent over in constant pain; it was quite theatrical. I never once stood erect but moved around bent at the waist. The platoon leader was disgusted with my condition and said, "Motherfucker, I would whip your ass if it wasn't for that telephone pole stuck up it." I just sloughed it off; I was workin' my plan.

Eventually, I was sent to the hospital. I was immediately admitted due to the extent of my pain and assigned a bed. Oh, my god, every bed was filled, and everybody in the infirmary had returned from Vietnam blown up like motherfuckers. It was horrible; most had at least one limb missing whereas others had multiple amputations. There must have been fifty soldiers in one large room. One soldier, two beds away from me, was missing both arms and both legs. Many times I was awakened in the middle of the night with his screams; if not his, someone else's. That was some fucked up shit!

My first day in the hospital, the doctor came in to examine me along with two medics. I was nervous to say the least. The doctor left after ordering traction for my bad back, and the medic installing the ropes and weights leaned over my bedside and said to me with disdain, "We know you are faking it." I was a bit stunned, of course, but from my research I was prepared for this "diagnosis." I knew they couldn't prove it. I was hooked up with all the traction apparatus and there I lay. I would simply try and stay as long as I could. Bring it on, motherfuckers!

Well, the rumor of my ruse spread to the other soldiers adjacent to me. Most significantly, the patient with no arms or legs shouted over, "Keep it up motherfucker, we are all behind you one hundred percent." He was one of many that made me aware of their sentiments. Sure I was scared, but this new support group of mine made my quest even more important. I couldn't let these guys down. They had been fucked badly for their loyalty and I wanted to shower them with mine. "Hell no, I won't go!"

After about a month of my alleged disability, the doctors still hadn't bought into it, so I was scheduled to be released from the hospital and returned to basic training. Apparently, I needed to come up with a new plan. A friend of mine got out of the Army by telling the authorities he was a homosexual. This, I'm afraid, was about to become my last-ditch effort; I wanted out.

I made an appointment to see the resident hospital chaplain. Oh, my god, this was going to be tough. However, I was committed. I walked into the chaplain's office and he addressed me with, "What can I do for you, soldier?" I said in response, "I've got a problem." He said, "Well, tell me what's your problem." With all the chutzpa I could garner, I said to him, "I'm a queer!" He said, "A what?" I could not believe I was going to have to say it twice, but I repeated, "A queer." I was astounded when he asked again, "A what?" This was the third fucking time I was going to have to call myself a queer and I was not very happy with how things were going. I then clearly stated, "I'm a homosexual!" Oh, fuck, how embarrassing; the words soured as they left my mouth. He replied, "Oh, you do have a problem." Whew, I thought that exchange would never end.

He then asked me to sit down and tell him about my issues. I told him it was difficult for me to be in the showers with so many naked men, blah, blah, blah. How totally humiliating, but I did what I had to do. He then informed me that he would help and asked me to return to his office a few days later. I was so fucking excited. I did it! I was going home!

Next I had to call my parents and give them the good news: "I'm coming home!" I did not allude to why or how I was coming home, only that it looked like I had a fairly good chance of doing so. Motherfucker, I heard the disappointment in their voices. I had been on the phone with them for maybe thirty minutes conversing back and forth when I realized how very proud they had been of my Army enlistment. I hung up and made my decision to stay. It would have been devastating for them to have their son leave San Antonio as a drug addict and return a homosexual. I couldn't do that to them, or to myself for that matter. Let's hit it; basic training here I come…again. I guessed I'd have to try some other exercise to keep me out of Vietnam.

After my return from the hospital, and into my third round of basic training, I had some funny experiences. One that always comes to mind occurred at the firing range. There was no way I wanted to be on the front lines with a gun in my hand in Vietnam. However, they issued everyone an M-16 rifle. You had to learn how to take it apart, clean it, and put it back together. Then they required you to learn how to shoot it. The drill sergeants would march the platoons over to the rifle range for target practice. They would spread all of us out in trenches, targets in front, and direct everyone to hit the bull's eye. We were expected to do our best; and everyone tried for that, except me. I knew better. There was no fucking way I was going to be considered a good marksman.

I never hit a single target, not in the upper corners, not the lower corners, not anywhere near. I made sure I never came close to the target whatsoever. The drill sergeants would stand over me yelling at the top of their lungs, "Stokes, you son of a bitch, hit the fucking target." These guys were yelling so hard the veins were popping out of their necks. They were in my face, from above, and to my side, sometimes two at a time. I was just sure they were eventually going to kick my fucking ass. I never hit one target, ever. They wanted to kill me!

After nine months and my third stint in basic training had passed, I finally graduated. I had by now pretty much figured out the way the Army operated. I was waiting on orders and just hanging out in the barracks on hold. I had scored some pot from someone on the base and kept it stashed behind the barracks in the woods. I would smoke a little and then return to the woods to hide my stash.

The meanest, I mean the meanest goddamned drill sergeant I had encountered throughout my lengthy triple-basic-training stay approached me one day and said, "Stokes, I know you are smoking weed and stashing it back in the woods behind the barracks. I've been watching you." I was flipping out and sure I was fucked. He then turned to me and said, "Do you think you could get me some LSD?" "You've got to be kidding!" I said incredulously. "No, no, no, I love that shit. Can you get us some?" "Us some?" I replied. "Yeah, seriously, I think this is the best man-made stuff on the planet," the drill sergeant confessed. I'll never forget those words. This mean motherfucking drill sergeant just said to me that he thought LSD was the best man-made stuff on the fucking planet! What planet was I on? How do I ever find these people, or better yet, how do they find me? My sister Lee has constantly posed the very same question to me my whole life.

So, of course, I scored us some LSD, and we took it together in the barracks multiple times during the night shift. On occasion, he would be assigned as the overnight duty officer and enlist me as his runner. We spent long nights together, all night and all fucked up on LSD. We became the best of friends. He invited me to his house to meet his wife and stay for dinner. He said I could spend the night, if so inclined. He lent me his Camaro, so I could tour Seattle, if I pleased. I attended some of the best rock concerts of my youth in Seattle due to his generosity. I saw the "Small Faces" with Rod Stewart, Ronnie Lane, and Ron Wood. I also saw the "Nitty Gritty Dirt Band," who was also popular at the time. It was ludicrous. Basic trainee recruits were never supposed to step outside the compound perimeter. You could be court-martialed. However, I had me a fucking Chevy Camaro!

My orders eventually came. I was to ship out to Fort Benjamin Harrison, Indianapolis, Indiana. The drill sergeant and

I said our good-byes, and off I went to Indianapolis. This was to be my next training facility. The Army refers to this as AIT, Advanced Individual Training. This is always the next step for recruits after basic training. I had landed in the pay distribution center for the Army, Navy, Marines, and Air Force. The Army had designated me to be a pay distribution clerk, and that was cool, but I didn't think I wanted to have to work that hard. It sounded like CPA work to me, like I would have to be doing math all day. I was horrible at math. However, I was not in Vietnam. I was safe, and that was most important. Nonetheless, as things progressed, it seemed as if my initial plan was continuing to unfold nicely.

I arrived in Indianapolis via bus and reported to the particular student company to which I was assigned, located on the grounds of Fort Benjamin Harrison. It was a beautiful campus. There were also girls stationed there. This was because Fort Ben Harrison housed all four of the military branches. This place was the banking center for the military as a whole. These girls weren't supermodels by any stretch of the imagination, but still they were girls. Hallelujah! I regret to report that during my stay, I had sex with only the lonely…although some were prettier than others. I felt that had to count for something.

I reported to my assigned student company and was required to go through the line with the other recruits to check in. I came to a second lieutenant who greeted our group and gathered a little data from each of us. He greeted me, and I offered my name and rank, "Corporal Sandy Stokes, reporting for duty, Sir." He offered his hand and shook mine. Then I leaned toward him and said quietly, "Sir, may I speak with you a moment?" He said, "Of course, corporal, what can I do for you?" I told him, "Sir, it's rather a long story, but I have now been in the Army going on nine months and I'm still not out of the training process."

He was shocked and said, "I have never heard of such a thing." I said, "I know, I know, and I will be happy to fill you in with the details later." As I was trying to figure out what details I could come up with, I said, "I'm pretty sick of the countless schools I have been attending and, by chance, might you have something I can do for you here without having to attend any additional schooling?" He turned to me and replied, "Well, maybe. Let me think about it and I'll call you in tomorrow."

Tomorrow came and over the loudspeaker I heard, "Stokes, report to Lieutenant McCaskill. Stokes, report to Lieutenant McCaskill immediately." Well, hell, you didn't have to ask me twice. I hurried down the staircase of my assigned barracks and stood at the door of his office at attention and saluted, "Corporal Stokes reporting, sir." He looked at me and said, "At ease, soldier. Won't you come in." I entered his office and stood there erect with my hands clasped behind my back and all of the military protocol I could conjure up. "Yes, sir," I responded. He looked up at me, smiled kindly, and asked, "How would you like to be the mail clerk for the student company here in our office?" I couldn't believe my fucking ears. I mean who the fuck wouldn't want to be the postman? I stood there in disbelief and said, "Yes, sir, I would be happy to accept the position." The Lieutenant replied, "Then report for duty at zero eight hundred hours tomorrow morning, and welcome aboard." "Thank you sir," I replied as I spun around in military fashion and exited his office. In my head, I was dancing out of his office thinking, "I'm the fucking postman, I'm the fucking postman!" It appeared all my efforts had paid off. I can assure you that going through basic training three separate times for nine months was no cakewalk, but I was safe and could breathe again.

The next day after acquiring the postman assignment, I was moved out of the student company and the multiple-bed barracks where recruits were mandated to stay. The student company recruits I was part of the day before now had to salute me, and follow any demands I might make. This was solely because I was now part of the staff, and as students, they had to follow orders. I was always nice, but I loved my new status. I had my own room with attached bath, apart from the students, all within a 24-hour period. My new room was huge, with multiple windows and twin beds. I put the twin beds together and made myself a king. Again, I hung Chinese lanterns from the ceiling. I got an Indian blanket for my king bed and I rummaged tables and chairs from adjoining suites. I had a friggin' love palace! I even had some of those lonely chicks I mentioned sneak in at night. Oh, my god, I was living the dream.

I became bolder and bolder with what I began to think of as my "private residence." I decided I would grow a little weed inside. The problem was it morphed into a lot of weed. I had more or less fifty little plants growing on trays lined up along the floor. It was a fucking greenhouse! This went on for about a month when one morning I was down in the office working in my mailroom, and the sergeant major, my new boss, was making polite conversation with me. He said, "Stokes, I hear your room is super spectacular the way you've fixed it up." I was feeling proud, until he said, "I even hear you're growing weed up there." Oh, my fucking god, I felt myself melt to a puddle on the floor! I pulled myself together as well as I could and answered, "Well, hell yes, sergeant major, doesn't everybody?" He snickered and with a smile walked back into his office. Again, I couldn't help thinking, "I'm so fucked!"

I sorted my mail faster than I had ever done before, and then I beelined, I ran, I sprinted, I may have even somersaulted out of the office and up to my room. I gathered the plants and containers as fast as I could and stuffed them all into trash bags.

Working furiously with sweat running down my face, I got all that shit together and to a dumpster off base, praying I had moved fast enough. Man oh man, what had I been thinking? This seemed to be a recurrent theme. Nothing more came of that episode, lucky enough. It was then I decided, with this defiant behavior of mine, it might be in my best interest to move off base. So I did.

My friend Lieutenant McCaskill had finished his tour of duty and was no longer at the camp to help buffer any resentments I may have created. My new boss was now the sergeant major. That same sergeant major was never too keen on my approach to Army life. I was always up front with my beliefs about the war in Vietnam and Army life as a career. I thought it was a cop-out. It was my conclusion that the Army was just a great place to hide out if you were afraid of making it in the real world. I don't feel that way anymore, because in hindsight, it had saved my ass, given me terrific income for an eighteen-year-old, and taught me more about life than any other circumstance available to a young man. Nonetheless, while I was there I was a complete and utter dissident. I was an upstream-swimming motherfucker! All one needed to do was ask, and I was always more than ready to speak my mind. That, apparently, was unacceptable behavior within this environment.

One day, I arrived at the mailroom and was locked out. Hmm…what the fuck was going on? Well, to my surprise, the sergeant major approached me at that moment and claimed a letter had been stolen. "A letter, are you kidding?" I was puzzled. "No, Stokes, not kidding," he said, as he stood there towering over me in his solemn and stern military style. I was perplexed as I looked up facing his imposing figure, and said, "Well, let me look for it." I proceeded to rummage through all of the mail placed in their slots after he'd let me back into my little office.

I was beginning to smell a setup. I knew this guy didn't like my style, but I was shocked—I didn't see this coming.

Unfortunately, this stolen letter thing blew into dynamic proportions. Before I knew it, the CID (Criminal Investigation Command) had me down in their offices under interrogation. I couldn't believe this shit. I had never stolen any mail, let alone this single fucking letter. The two officers with the CID, however, wanted to search my car and apartment in downtown Indianapolis. "I'm cool with that," I told them, knowing all along I did not have the letter and never did. They searched my car with no results and then wanted to follow me to my apartment in separate cars. In my usual obsequious manner, I responded, "Why of course, please follow me," because these guys were the military's version of the FBI. How else was I supposed to react? They were both extremely polite, because the FBI is always extremely polite before they bust your fucking ass.

Well, my apartment was another "den of iniquity." First of all, it was an efficiency, four hundred square feet total living area at best. I had a twenty-some odd pipe collection displayed on the wall above my bed. My bed was a mattress on the floor, adorned with an Indian style blanket, and the walls were plastered with Jimi Hendrix and Grateful Dead posters. It resembled a hippie crash pad, just the way I had designed it to look. The worst part was I had ten pounds of weed in an Army duffle sack under my kitchen sink. Things were looking mighty grim as I watched them in my rearview mirror following me to my pad. What the fuck was I going to do? Again, I just knew this was my death march.

We arrived together, and I walked them down three concrete steps to my front door. "I am so fucked," I said a thousand times in my head. We entered the apartment with my pipe collection in brilliant display, and they proceeded to search my apartment. "Oh fuck, oh fuck, oh fuck," I repeated to myself with heart pounding. However, most importantly, I continued to look and act cool. Within sixty seconds, one of them approached and opened the cupboard doors under the sink. He looked in and around briefly, moved the gunnysack out of the way to see behind it, and closed the cupboard doors just as gently and quietly as he had opened them. I couldn't fucking believe it!

Well, you would have thought I was goddamned Tinker Bell the way I flickered around after that, saying to them, "Now let's look in here, or in here, or maybe in here! Here's the bathroom, let's look in here." I couldn't have been more helpful or accommodating. From my behavior, they could have been a couple of long lost, dear friends, who had left something behind and were in dire need of finding it. They finally wrapped up their investigation, and off they went. Damn, once again, couldn't fucking believe it! I was stupefied!

Regardless of not finding the single missing letter, the sergeant major now had grounds to transfer me. I was terrified of what might be ahead. Damn, I shouldn't have been so obviously the quintessential hippie. Unfortunately, it was simply my character to be who I was, regardless of the circumstances. Time to face the consequences. I had been ousted. The sergeant major had exiled me to the mess hall. Once again, I just knew I was fucked.

As luck would have it, the mess hall was an even better place to work. I became the clerk in charge of ordering all the food and creating the menu. The cooking staff all worked underneath me and would bring me their fresh-baked pies and delicious entrées, all in hopes of patronizing me. The sergeant major thought he was demoting me when he was actually giving me a raise. I thought I was king of men!

I spent the remainder of my Army career as the head clerical for the mess hall and had the time of my life. I drove into base every morning in my Army greens, flying along in my Fiat, maybe with the top down. When I arrived, I sorted a few deliveries, created the menu for the week, ate some pie, and was out of there by noon for the remainder of the day. I was nineteen-and-one-half years old, and life was treating me pretty well. I'm afraid I was becoming a legend in my own mind.

Tragedy struck one day, however, when I received the news that Stevie had died. He had overdosed on Quaaludes. He had taken too many, which was not necessarily uncommon for either one of us; but this time it went too far. He was barely nineteen years old. I was devastated and could not begin to comprehend the extent of the loss. I was grief-stricken for months. This guy meant more to me than anybody else in the world.

Ironically, I eventually began to realize I was free to choose my own path as a result of this loss. Though I felt disloyal for those thoughts, I knew that was the only way for me to survive. Loyalty juxtaposed with survival; I chose the latter. Stevie and I had lost our other *compadre* and running mate Gary to similar circumstances, shortly before I shipped off to the Army. I would be flying solo from here on out. The Army and my subsequent epiphany about Stevie had apparently saved my life. Thank God for my father's foresight.

I must admit, even though my father saved me from my friends' grim fate, I still continued my unorthodox lifestyle as a young adult and assuredly let him down more times than I care to admit. Yet, his example always offered me a great point of reference, and has kept me grounded throughout my life. Unfortunately, I was unaware and indifferent to his influence until much later in life. I was still a motherfucking Terrell Hills cowboy, an outlaw with something to prove and lawlessness flowing through my veins. I would not be contained. I had less than zero regard for consequence and proved it time and time again. My father, however, continued to support me as his son and offered me nothing but love. I don't know how the fuck he did it.

Approximately one year after my release from active duty, I received a letter in the mail requiring me to return to the nearest military base for an additional two-week stint. I would have to wear my Army greens, boots, and hat. I was freaked out because by then I had let my hair grow long again, and in no way did I want to cut it back to military standards. So I made a call. I asked if I could wear a wig for the upcoming two weeks once reporting to Fort Sam Houston. I was told I could.

I was greatly relieved, but now I had to find a wig. I found one that had belonged to our cleaning lady. Oddly, it was wadded up in the back of my sister's closet. It was a short, platinum-blonde wig, and a cheap one at that. The white, silvery hair resembled bad doll hair: pure nylon and pure fake. It would have to work. I secured my hair up with bobby pins and slipped it on. Oh, my god, this stupid wig was hysterical looking. It resembled a Halloween disguise and would fool no one. I could only hope it would look better once I cut it to military standards. Easy. I would have my buddy, a nonprofessional barber, take a pair of scissors and work his magic. He did his best, given his lack of skill and my unsolicited assistance. Neither of us had ever cut hair, let alone a wig, and it showed. I looked ridiculous. However, I reported for duty nonetheless, proud in my starched uniform and "military" haircut.

Strangely, I never heard a word about my appearance from anyone in the office the whole two weeks I worked there. They acted like they didn't even notice, as if I were a cancer patient and they were afraid they might offend me. I was down with that; I didn't say anything either. However, when returning from lunch my last day on base, I passed a first lieutenant and forgot to salute him. He stopped me and said curtly, "Specialist, where's my salute?" Bewildered by his demand, I apologetically responded, "Excuse me sir," and saluted him immediately. He looked at me and said, "Take off your hat, specialist." I removed the wedge cap I had balanced on top of my wig. Once I did that, he grabbed the wig off my head and while holding it in his hand said, "Now what the hell is this, soldier?" I looked back at him with my pinned up hair and said, "Sir, I am only here on reserve status and this was all approved before I came." "Present your ID, soldier," he demanded. I handed over my new military ID, solemnly depicting me in my maid's wig. He then said in very guttural disgust, "Yuck!" and threw the wig and ID at my feet while he marched off. Over all, I had a pretty good time those two weeks.

CHAPTER THREE

Doctor, doctor, I feel so bad
This is the worst day, I ever had
Have you this misery a very long time?
If you have, I'll lay it on the line

You've gotta put on your sailin' shoes
Put on your sailin' shoes
Everyone will hip hooray
When you put on your sailin' shoes
Put on your sailin'—put on your sailin' shoes

… *"Sailin' Shoes" by Lowell George*

I was released from the Army in mid-1971, six months early, to allow a return to college. This was standard procedure during the Vietnam era, regardless of where you were stationed. You only needed to apply. I spent a year and a half in the Army and then was on my way home. I returned to Texas to attend the University of Texas in Austin. It appeared Austin had an even worse drug problem than the one I had experienced in San Antonio. However, I was nineteen years old, and it fit me like a glove. Apparently, "old habits die hard."

Not surprisingly, school didn't work out so well for me in Austin. I passed my classes but just barely. I had little interest. I made my first run to the border during this time and was hooked before I knew it. Could smuggling be my future? I made money, I could buy more drugs, and the chicks were abundant. Nope, school was not working out for me. Who needed it? What I needed, I concluded, was to move to Mexico. I could be king of the wild frontier! I was always very convincing, even to myself.

I dropped out of UT and moved back to San Antonio briefly. I had no job of consequence and was surrounded by the use of heroin. All of my friends were doing it, and I was as well. It became obvious there was very little future for me there. I let my parents know I needed to get out of town and process Stevie's death. This was fact; I missed him immensely, but again, did not want to follow in his footsteps. It was treacherous terrain ahead. I had learned something from his demise: it would be death and destruction were I to stick around. Mexico was calling.

I settled my pending responsibilities and packed a bag. Then my mother, bless her heart, drove me to the train station in Laredo with her friend Mrs. Berkowitz. I hadn't a clue where I was going when I stepped onto that train. I had my backpack and maybe a thousand dollars and headed south. I was barely twenty years old and couldn't have imagined I would never return to San Antonio to live.

The trip was incredible. I rode trains and buses and hitchhiked around the entire country of Mexico for about six months. These were more casual times, when hitchhiking was less dangerous, and Mexico more sympathetic in its embrace of a foreigner. I was a curiosity to the Mexicans with my *guero* looks, but I was young, harmless, and approachable. I moved around Mexico easily. I slept in cheap motels, flop houses, and hammocks, making my money go a long way. I ate food from the street vendors and happily engaged in conversation in broken Spanish. However, I soon started to pick up the language and eventually became conversational, opening even more doors. I met plenty of other foreigners from multiple countries as well. I tried to see everything and go everywhere. I traveled from coast to coast, Mazatlan to Merida. I went to Cancun when it was a barren desert, just a beach. I saw the ruins in Palenque and slept in my hammock for weeks along the river. I went to the ruins in Oaxaca, the ruins in Tulum. I even went to Belize; baby, I went all over!

On my way back north heading toward the border, I stopped in the town of Cholula, Puebla, just southeast of Mexico City. Kip, a high school friend of mine, was attending the University of the Americas in this small town. It was immediately obvious to me that there was something a little different about Cholula. There were pretty girls of every nationality strolling down the streets. Where the hell was I—paradise?

Kip had a small house near the university and immediately welcomed me, inviting me to stay with him. He was built like a football player but dressed in white Oaxacan clothing. Kip had platinum blond hair, which he wore in a long ponytail. He was very calm and casual, and his life seemed totally alluring. Soon, his roommate showed up with a huge gunnysack of peyote. Was I dreaming? I was completely blown away with this casual Mexican lifestyle.

After a few joints and a night's sleep, Kip encouraged me to tour the university while he attended his classes. He left me alone to hang around by myself. I sat cross-legged on the lawn in the middle of campus surveying the new surroundings. I saw the most incredibly diverse group of people. There were all ethnicities routinely going about their business. I was particularly taken by the most beautiful Asian chick I had ever seen in my life. This must be the place I belonged. Without hesitation, I made a commitment at that exact moment: "I'm going back to school." I wanted absolutely nothing to do with my previous life; I wanted Kip's!

And that's just what I got. I called my parents to get their approval to attend college in Cholula. They were both so overjoyed that I would even consider going back to school that they readily agreed. The GI Bill would help pay for my schooling along with the assistance from my grandmother and parents. There was no looking back; I lived in Cholula.

The town of Cholula was nestled quietly at the base of two active, snow-capped volcanoes named Popocatepetl and Iztaccihuatl. It was a breathtaking setting and the university campus was absolutely beautiful. The school had a crazy mix of faculty and students from around the world, but mainly wealthy Mexicans and curious Americans like me. In the center of town was a remarkable third-century pre-Columbian pyramid, the largest in the world, with thousands of years of history attached. There was more to do and see around Cholula than I had ever dreamed.

To be practical, I moved into an apartment with a local family, the Alvarezes, who shared their complex with me. It was still private, an upstairs unit with kitchen, living room, bath, and bedroom. We shared an entrance into a small courtyard from the street, and then it was up a flight of stairs to my apartment. I also had my own balcony that overlooked the main thoroughfare coming into Cholula. I could hear the noisy, speeding buses with diesel engines spewing out exhaust and the attendant screaming, "Puebla, Puebla!" It was heaven on earth.

The family was extremely welcoming to their new American college student. I was invited for meals, if I so chose, but they were never intrusive. They gave me my first introduction to *Mole Pueblano*, renowned for its origins in the state of Puebla. The taste was completely foreign to me, yet alluring. Regretfully, in its original form, I've always thought it resembled a large block of dried blood. Sick as that may sound, it was simply delicious. The Alvarezes introduced me to many other Mexican dishes as well, completely different from the Tex Mex menu I was familiar with in San Antonio.

After six months of traveling on my own and then living with the Alvarezes, my Spanish began to improve immensely. I was also taking Spanish classes in college. The locals were always questioning me about where I was from, because I looked so *gringo* yet my Spanish had become fluent. I was somewhat of an anomaly to them. (A crazy footnote is that my seventh-grade Spanish teacher had told my mother, "Sandy is incapable of learning a foreign language." I hated seventh-grade Spanish and I hated that demanding bitch!)

Oh, man, I had some fun fooling the locals with my Spanish. One time, I was walking home around midnight from Tio Wilos, a popular college hangout, when I stopped to buy a *gordita* from one of the local street venders. There was a group of Mexican guys standing around and waiting their turn. One of them turned to the group and said in Spanish with disdain, "Look at this fucking punk; this piece of *gringo* shit. Who the fuck does he think he is?" I turned to them with a smile and said in perfect Spanish, "Just like you brother, right?" These guys were shocked and embarrassed at being caught and responded with camaraderie, "No, *amigo*. We were just talking trash, please excuse us." You would have thought we were long lost brothers.

By this time, I had become comfortable with my surroundings and felt part of Cholula. I had been encouraging a girl I cared about in high school to come and visit. Her name was Kathy, a green-eyed knockout with a perfect figure. We had been in constant contact, and hell, I missed her. Kathy had been modeling in New York City while I had been busy finding myself in Mexico. I liked this girl a lot.

Kathy arrived in the small Mexican village of Cholula wearing all of her New York City chic. By then, I was deeply into my Oaxacan peasant clothing, which consisted of white cotton pullover shirts and white drawstring pants with leather huaraches sandals that had soles made from tires. My mindset had also become Oaxacan, very casual and somewhat spiritual. I thought I was "beyond cool." Therefore, this outfit thing was creating a lot of mixed feelings for me. The dichotomy was simply absurd, and I was having issues with the cultural contrast. I really liked this chick, but damn, couldn't she dress down a little? As we walked the streets together, there she was in mini skirts and revealing tops, sauntering along in her black and shiny high-heeled shoes, "click, click, click, click" over the cobblestones. "We're in Cholula girl. Barefoot would have been better than this," I thought to myself.

We were both young, however, and struggling to establish our new identities, maybe even showing off a little for each other. In retrospect, what guy wouldn't want a top New York City model hanging on his arm, regardless of his station in life or where he was in the world? My struggle was with who I had become since our last rendezvous. I think I may have been a bit rude, even though she was only visiting and by my invitation. What a dog I was. We did get the chance to meet up in Europe years later and I came away infatuated…but that time she got to blow me off. It was well deserved.

As I have mentioned, Cholula had an eclectic mix of people, my kind of people. The hippie movement was still underway; the time, mid-1973. I made friends easily; one in particular was David. We were the same age and, coincidentally, he was from San Antonio's north side, a graduate of MacArthur High School. He had long, dark, shoulder-length hair, smoked a ton of weed, and was a guitar player. I fancied myself a guitar player as well. I had a D-35 Martin that Stevie's mother had given me after his passing. It was one of the best guitars made and meant everything to me. The fact that I had a Martin made me appear a much better player than I actually was. I had a Martin! That alone impressed the shit out of David.

David and I soon became inseparable. We practiced our guitars together in my little apartment, sometimes up to seven hours a day. We smoked weed as much; in fact, so much, we were at risk of spontaneous combustion. It was Mexico, the birthplace of weed as far as we were concerned. We went to school, smoked weed, and played our guitars. We eventually formed a band, The Russ Stokes Group, featuring Lightning Wes Carver. It was only the two of us. We started playing all the local bars in and around town and, on occasion, at the university. After a while, we actually started to envision ourselves as rock stars.

In Cholula, the culture was "free love" due to women's liberation and the introduction of the birth control pill. Sex was alive and well. All inhibitions were kicked to the curb. AIDS had yet to surface. The birth control pill had become the catalyst for the sexual revolution. Just so happened, I was in the right place at the right time. It was chicks for nothing and drinks for free. Girls were falling all over us. I came close to sleeping with a different girl nearly every night for two years running. It was ridiculous. After a while, I couldn't remember whom I had or hadn't slept with. I was further becoming a legend in my own mind.

One night, David and I were in his old, red Ford truck driving down Main Street headed toward the university, most likely on our way to Tio Wilos to get a White Russian, one of our favorite drinks at the time. We came upon the railroad crossing just after the pyramid and looked down the tracks to see if a train was coming. There were no alerts at the crossings in Mexico as we were accustomed to in the States. Damn, a train was barreling down the tracks as we ground to a halt. We had stopped, literally, in the nick of time…or so we thought.

As the train came speeding and lumbering through the intersection, we suddenly realized we had stopped too close. Incredibly, it was hitting our bumper, "kaboom, kaboom, kaboom," with every passing car. We were both plastered to the seat in utter fear. We just knew we were about to be yanked down the tracks any minute by that ripping train. We were completely freaked out, and I was shouting over the roar of the train, "Put it in reverse motherfucker, put this motherfucker in reverse!" David was scared out of his mind and worried that if he put the clutch in, we might roll even further ahead and be pulled under the moving train.

I couldn't appreciate his concern at first and continued to yell, "Put the motherfucker in reverse, goddammit!" The train this whole time was smacking against the bumper, "kaboom, kaboom, kaboom," with indescribable force and resonance, and we were vibrating from the multiple impacts. We were totally freaked-fucking-out when David eventually got his truck in reverse, and we slowly inched away. We were both white with fear. Never in my life had I been so close to being killed. We may have laughed about it later, but cautiously, as that was one of the scariest moments either of us had ever experienced, and that is no shit!

I soon learned that the pharmacies in and around Cholula were wide open and that without a prescription, I could buy Quaaludes, Mandrex, and Hycodan, a codeine-infused pill much like Vicodin sold in the States; Jesus Christ, it was better than owning a pharmacy and without the fixed overhead costs. I figured this out early. Hell, I could have been a pharmacist with all the data I had acquired.

As you may imagine, I loved and abused all. I discovered I could buy ten thousand Quaaludes at a time for ten cents a piece and carry them to the States, selling them for one dollar each. Can you imagine telling a pharmacist, "I want to buy ten to twenty thousand Quaaludes" and their response, "Come by tomorrow and I will have your order ready"? It was as simple as that! The profit was incredible: roughly ten times your investment for each individual tablet. Do the math: $1,000 would turn into $10,000 and $2,000 would become $20,000. Who the fuck wouldn't want to make that kind of money? All I knew was…I did. Motherfucker, it was a cash cow, and I exploited it!

Sex, drugs, and rock 'n' roll became my complete and utter focus. I started buying weed in larger and larger quantities. I was convinced it was time to start taking it to the States. I was still in my little apartment at the Alvarezes' house when I began to sneak bales and bales of weed up into my flat. I had met another student named Mike whom I discovered was moving small quantities of weed to the States. I asked him, "Do you think if I followed you back to Texas, you could help me to get some of my weed across the border?" To my surprise he answered, "Of course, I'm happy to help…for a fee." Shitfire, damn, I had always been about paying my own way, and I quickly replied, "Well, hell yes, more than happy to!"

Along with the pills, this weed marked the beginning of my long and fruitful smuggling career. Within a year, at the age of twenty-two and still residing with this unsuspecting family, I had moved enough weed to the States to have made close to one million dollars. Crazy!

With all of my newfound cash, I decided to take twelve of my closest friends to a Rolling Stones concert in San Antonio. I had purchased front-row seats for everyone. When I passed though customs in Dallas, Texas, I had ten thousand Quaaludes in my socks, still in their wrappers. I made it through and all was cool. However, when I went to board the plane for San Antonio, they had these newly installed metal detectors. I was not prepared for that. As I passed through the arch, it went off, "beep, beep, beep," The fucking foil wrappers! The attendant said to me, "Sir, I'm sorry, but could you pass though the metal detector again for me? I'm sorry for the inconvenience." Well shit, I knew what was activating the detector, the damn Quaaludes! I casually turned towards the attendant and said, "Why of course, but may I go to the bathroom right quick? I'll be right back." These machines were a new addition to airport security, and therefore, the attendants were not yet so strict. He replied, "Well, of course, sir. We will wait for you here." Unheard of today, but fortunately, that was when there was still a bit of courtesy between the passengers and security.

I stumbled into the bathroom, alarmed at my new predicament, and tried to figure out what the fuck I was gonna do. I had twelve people meeting me in San Antonio, and I could not afford to miss the plane, but this was $10,000. I was undecided about my next move, particularly since I had walked them through customs OK, and that was an even a bigger deal. However, these new metal detectors had now created an additional hurdle.

My options were limited. I couldn't take ten thousand pills out of their wrappers and still catch my plane, so I decided, "Oh well, got to do what I got to do." I took my loaded socks down to a trashcan in the parking lot and tossed them in. I confidently strode back to the awaiting metal detector for my non-alerting walk through and boarded the plane. "*C'est la vie!*" I had bigger plans; there was a Rolling Stones concert to attend.

A few weeks later, I was strolling the streets of Cholula and sipping on a smoothie from one of the local *licuado* shops. Nothing out of the ordinary, just walking along when my smuggling friend Mike pulled up in his van. This van was full of tit dancers from Texas, apparently girlfriends of his, down on vacation. Well, shit, these girls were over-the-top, already drunk, and it was only nine in the morning. They jumped out of the van and swooped down on me like locusts, "Hey motherfucker, you're cute as a button. Get your young ass in the van and right now!" Next thing I knew, I was in the van and they were flashing their tits at me and rubbing them in my face. They were, basically, having their way with me as only tit dancers know how. I started to enjoy myself immediately. Hell, I was only grabbing a smoothie, and now this?

These chicks were crazy! I had never encountered anything like them. Honestly, even though I was a little crazy myself, I had never seen the inside of a tit bar in my life. I guess you could say I was somewhat naïve when it came to this kind of overt female seduction. "Ouwee!" and off we went speeding toward Taxco, a silver-mining community southwest of Cholula. I had been kidnapped.

The next thing I knew, after downing shot after shot after shot of tequila, I was in Taxco with these femme fatales from Texas sporting only cowboy hats. Texas women, I have got to say, have a tendency to be a bit on the wild side. At least, these adorable darlin's were, and I mean that literally, shirtless and braless the whole way. They were leaning out the windows, shouting "Yahoo!" and mooning the passing traffic, keeping me naked most of the way as well. I was having a blast, I don't mind sayin'. I was a little surprised at their conservativeness when they put their clothes back on to rent the hotel rooms. I was still captive, however, and a victim as far as I was concerned. Apparently, they liked me; maybe they would let me live. I would have to stay cool and adhere to my captors' requests, nonetheless.

I survived the next three days of total debauchery, and afterward they released me back to the streets of Cholula, weak, bleary-eyed, and hung over. They then peeled their tires and sped away, still shirtless and braless, back to Texas, yet to sober up. This was one of my first true encounters with exaggerated sex, drugs, and rock 'n' roll. No telling what happened to those girls. Glad I don't know.

Up till now, I was still living in that apartment with the Alvarez family, and it was beginning to get very uncool. I had an abundance of respect for them and didn't want to offend them in anyway. My lifestyle was completely foreign to them, and I was worried about the risk of bringing so much weed into their home. I loved this family who had been willing to accept such a crazy fucking gringo. I realized I could be putting them in harm's way. I needed a new pad.

I found one on the outskirts of town that fit the necessary requirements. It was private, a stucco structure with a courtyard and adjacent living quarters. I moved in sometime in 1974 and lived there about a year. Since I was rich by then, I even hired a maid. I had a truck, a stereo, an abundance of record albums, and several guitars, all the amenities that made for a comfortable life in Cholula. I was still attending classes "to the best of my ability," but my focus was now on the money.

One day, I was making my way up Popocatepetl and saw a large ranch-style home with a *se renta* sign posted and jotted down the number. Once back in town, I stopped at the local phone center to place a call to the *señor a*nd owner of the property. No one in the town of Cholula, at that time, had a telephone. Everybody had to go to the phone center to place any local or long-distance calls. Incredibly, I ended up renting the ranch, one of the biggest places in Cholula. It belonged to the mayor: five bedrooms, six baths, a fireplace, a private telephone, and a bathtub; all nonexistent and unheard of in the entire surrounding area. The mayor had moved into town, whereas I, on the other hand, definitely needed to stay out of town.

This ranch was so extravagant that I became quite the kingpin. It was very prestigious and alluring for someone of my young age to have such a big ranch and that soon became part of my persona. One day, consumed with my big-shot attitude, I complained to the mayor, my landlord, "*Oye*, I'm paying the highest rent in the entire state of Puebla!" and he simply responded with, "I know." How was I supposed to challenge that? He must've been aware of all the traffic in and out of my compound. I had two girls living with me, numerous smuggled motorcycles parked all around, and vehicles coming and going at all hours. This made my quest for reduced rent simply a nonissue from the mayor's point of view. He left me with absolutely no argument, so I continued to pay the rent he requested. Life was magnificent at that old ranch. I was beginning to love college!

CHAPTER FOUR

I've been from Tucson to Tucumcari
Tehachapi to Tonapah
Driven every kind of rig that's ever been made
Now I've driven the back roads so I wouldn't get weighed
And if you give me: weed, whites, and wine
And you show me a sign
I'll be willin', to be movin'

... *"Willin'" by Lowell George*

Even as quiet as I had been trying to keep it, rumors had begun to surface that I was smuggling weed back into Texas. Since I'd moved to the ranch in 1975, the loads had become larger and the trips to Texas more frequent. However, there was nothing easy about any of this. It all started in the mountains of Oaxaca, Mexico. Ricardo was my weed connection. He was Oaxacan, a tall, good-looking guy with jet-black, slicked-back hair; a real ladies' man, the kind of guy you would expect to see in this line of work. Incredibly, he was also from a well-to-do family. His father was a doctor. I went to Sunday dinners at Ricardo's and conversed with his sisters and parents. Nothing out of the ordinary, except for the lifestyle Ricardo and I led: fast motorcycles, fast trucks, fast women, and a career in smuggling. Nothing out of the ordinary, like I said.

Ricardo's family had a summer home in Puerto Angel on the coast of Oaxaca, bordering the Pacific. We spent many weekends at that location. We left Oaxaca, generally on speeding motorcycles, for the eight-hour ride to Puerto Angel through mountainous terrain, smoking twenty to thirty joints along the way. Plain and simple, this was nothing out of the ordinary.

Ricardo's job was to secure the weed from the growers in the surrounding mountains. It should be noted that the weed was not supplied by one grower with a big field of marijuana, but rather multiple peasant farmers from various villages throughout the hills of Oaxaca and the surrounding area. Ricardo's job was to coordinate the various peasants to compile the thousand pounds necessary to complete one load. A standard truck could only hold this amount. Sometimes this took months to accumulate. We always wanted the best, and the best took some time.

Next, we had to transfer the weed from the peasants to my truck and then ride out of the mountains at midnight. This was, without a doubt, one of the more hair-raising aspects of the entire operation. I never knew what I was driving into as I climbed the dark mountain trails late at night for an hour or more, deep into the mountains of Oaxaca, alone in my pickup. Once I arrived at the predestined spot, twenty or more peasants would emerge from the shadows, each with his WWI or WWII-styled rifle in his hands, converging on the truck. It was downright terrifying. There was always a bit of chaos during the exchange there in the middle of the night, but the money would be disbursed, approximately $80,000 in cash. Once the payment was concluded and the back of the pickup truck loaded, I then hauled ass back down the mountain, happy to still have my life intact. I must admit, however, I thrived on the fear…all of it.

Boch (pronounced "Bosh") was Ricardo's partner. He was an amazing guy, an accomplished artist from Bulgaria with an astonishing life story. His self-taught Spanish was extremely fluent. He spoke and understood Spanish better than the Mexicans themselves. I first noticed Boch while I was having coffee in the town center of Oaxaca City, waiting to meet Ricardo. Boch towered above the Mexicans at six foot three with a large, exaggerated European mustache and goatee. I stood out as well with long, blond hair and a *guero* appearance. Coincidentally, we found ourselves together in Ricardo's apartment later that day where the weed smoke was billowing and the conspiracy forming. We were both caught by surprise by each other's presence and instantly became friends. From that day forward, Boch acted as the liaison between Ricardo and me.

Sometime later, Boch and I traveled back to Oaxaca to complete a deal. As we were checking into a hotel, he suddenly broke into a foreign language with an older couple that had arrived at the same time. I left him at the counter blabbing away in an unrecognizable tongue. Later, he came to our room and informed me the older couple was Russian, and that he, of course, spoke the language perfectly. I was blown away. I then learned he was also fluent in French and Italian, besides English, Spanish, and his native language of Bulgarian.

Boch and I spent a lot of time together, always engaging in lengthy intellectual and philosophical discussions involving our two understandings of the world. He was very informed. Americans know next to nothing about Eastern European history, current or past. I was continuously humbled by Boch. I learned a lot from him and I hope he learned from me as well. From his view, I was a privileged white boy from Terrell Hills and an easy target of resentment. However, during my short life I had developed insight and compassion through my exposure to other cultures. This was the time of the "Ugly American," and I only hoped I represented an alternative persona.

I could write an entire book on Boch's life alone. As mentioned, he was an incredible artist as well as a renegade intellectual. Boch had grown up a wealthy capitalist in Bulgaria before the Russians overtook his country and stole the preserves factory his grandfather had built. The local school kids ridiculed him for his affluent upbringing. He was taunted by fellow classmates on a field trip to what had been his grandfather's factory and was now owned by the state.

Boch had fled Bulgaria as a teenager, while the country was still under a Communist regime. He made it to Cuba on his wits alone. From Cuba he was able to travel to Mexico City without raising any flags with the Communists. He had been instrumental in getting his parents out of Bulgaria and into Cuba and then to Mexico City. Incredibly, his father had been a famous boxer with credentials similar to those of Muhammad Ali.

Once Boch arrived in Mexico with portfolio in hand, it became easy to convince the head of the Art Department of the University of Mexico that he was a Guggenheim Award recipient. Boch had a terrific line of bullshit and yet the credentials that could withstand any scrutiny in the world of art. He was accepted to the University of Mexico, which allowed him the alibi and residence papers to bring his parents to Mexico. He was a fascinating guy.

With Boch and Ricardo as my connections, the procurement of weed in Oaxaca ran smooth as silk. However, Mike and his gang, who were crossing my weed, started stealing portions of my load, if not the whole thing. Fucking smugglers—some had ethics, others did not. This went with the territory. These guys were bottom feeders. Therefore, I broke away from them and hooked up directly with the Mexicans who had been crossing both of our loads. These guys owned ranches that bordered both sides of the Rio Grande River that divided Matamoros and Brownsville. This was some slick shit, and at night the Mexicans would just take my weed and walk it across from one ranch to the other. Not really very sophisticated, but it worked. The next day I would pick the load up in the little town of San Benito, just north of the border.

In order to transport my weed to the States, it was critical to have a good mechanic I could rely on. I found one in Austin who became another great friend. His name was Clark, a tall, lanky fellow with a thick mop of hair. I called him my resident Einstein. He was incredibly skilled and had the hands of a magician. As far as I could tell, he could wave his wand over any motor or mechanical part and anything that had been broken was fixed, perfectly. The guy was brilliant. At some point, he added multiple hidden gas tanks to my vehicle and strategically placed a single control knob within arm's reach. This allowed me to transfer from tank to tank and never have to stop for fuel, giving me close to a thousand mile range. This configuration screamed "Thunder Road" from the late fifties film. My blessed '68 Dodge truck, christened the "Dream Machine," never let me down as she outpaced many Mexican cop cars on the rides north to the US.

While speeding toward the border with my truck full of weed, I routinely encountered Mexican checkpoints. There would be one or two low-ranking military personnel standing in front of a shack that served as their station. They could see me coming from a distance...and I could see them. As I approached, they would wave their arms in an attempt to pull me over for a check of my papers and the contents of my truck. I wasn't having anything to do with that. I was rollin'! These dumbasses had no radios or chase vehicles and would be standing in the middle of the highway waving at me like clowns, causing me to press my gas pedal to the floor. "Motherfuckers, I would suggest you get the fuck out of my way, if you don't want to end up like flattened armadillos."

They would watch me getting closer and closer in my classic Ray-Ban shades, grasping the steering wheel while peering though my windshield until I was upon them. I would then press the gas pedal even harder, pushing it beyond a hundred miles per hour, making them dive to the shoulders of the road in fear amidst all the spraying gravel. I would look at their blur through my driver's-side window as I passed, smiling and waving. "*Adios* motherfuckers," I would murmur to myself as I watched them in my rearview mirror, scrambling back to the center of the road, still waving as if I hadn't seen them.

Once I got the weed across the border through my new Mexican partners, the next obstacle was getting it through the immigration checkpoint on the way to Austin. I was doing some ballsy shit getting my loads through the Sarita checkpoint, a hundred miles north of the Texas/Mexico border. Sarita was the only immigration stop on Highway 77 coming out of the South Texas Valley. Its purpose was to check for illegal immigrants. For the normal American citizen it was a breeze, just a mandatory immigration stop—so what? In South Texas these stops were commonplace. For me, however, there were huge consequences if things didn't go so well. In my business, I always had to be prepared for them. At these checkpoints, border patrol agents would stop every car headed north and ask the driver to roll down the window, and then present the question, "Good afternoon, are you an American citizen?" During this brief interaction, they would look the driver and any passengers sternly in the eyes and wait for a response, all the while making short glances surveying the inside of the vehicle, staying focused on everyone's demeanor.

It was a cat and mouse game. "If I can catch you, by god, I'm going to." It was their job. They may have even asked the driver to open the trunk, all the while maintaining eye-to-eye contact. They were looking for any semblance of suspicious behavior. They would assess the situation car by car. The appropriate response was of course, "Yes, sir." Normally, the agent would then step away from the vehicle and proceed to flag the car on through. With eight hundred to a thousand pounds of weed in the back of my truck, this would be the exact response I was hoping to hear. "Move on through, son" was like a gift from God.

I remember going through the Sarita checkpoint in the Dream Machine during the early days of my smuggling career. At the time, I had shoulder-length hair and wore Oaxacan shirts, with dark heroin-style sunglasses. I fit the profile of a suspected trafficker to a "T," especially with my older truck and hippie appearance. However, I had become a student of the human psyche, especially when it came to border patrol agents. That was my job, dammit. I had concluded that if I looked liked the consummate drug smuggler, I could use it as my guise. I used this approach to my advantage. Who the fuck would be stupid enough to have an eight-hundred-pound load of weed in the back of his pickup truck, looking the way I did? I just knew this was some clever shit. However, I also had stupid fucking luck, regardless of how clever I thought I was.

One time, there were three cars ahead of me when I rolled to a stop at the Sarita checkpoint. "Yeah, baby, profile me, motherfucker!" Shit, the border agent took one look at me, and waved all three of the cars ahead right on through without stopping. He was focused on me. He kept his eyes sternly on mine and signaled me to move ahead. As I rolled to a stop, he approached my window. I dutifully rolled it down, as he stared hard at me. I casually removed my shades, and stared directly back. It was eye-to-eye contact now—game on! I was confident and scared simultaneously. I looked back at him with blue eyes bright and clear and said, "Yes, sir?" He seemed a little surprised once I had removed my heroin shades, and asked, "Are you an American citizen?" scrutinizing me carefully. "Yes, sir, I am," I replied cheerfully. He asked again, "Where are you going and what's in the back?" I responded, "I am moving out of South Texas on my way to college in Austin, and these are my belongings in the back, sir." I knew my etiquette. He walked around the truck surveying my exterior and cargo, waiting for me to exhibit some form of suspicious behavior. Uh-huh, he was doing his job, and I, on the other hand, was doing mine. He circled my truck and authoritatively appeared back at the driver's side window. Then he said to me, "Drive safely, and have a nice day." Wow, had I called this one right? I was stunned. I thought to myself, "I'm getting fucking good at this shit. *Adios*, motherfuckers!"

I got to Austin after driving all night. It was about six in the morning when I arrived downtown. Incredibly, an Austin cop pulled behind me and with lights flashing, directed me to pull over. Motherfucker, no fucking way! I was fucked; eight hundred pounds in the back and I looked like shit. Here I was again being pulled over with my long fucking hair, Mexican garb, and dark shades, plus I had been up all night; Jesus fucking Christ, what the fuck now? The cop walked up to my driver's window and said, "Son, I guess you are wondering why I pulled you over?" With the best coherent face I could put on, I said, "Yes, sir, was I speeding?" "No, son, you were weaving," the cop explained. "Really, weaving, eh?" I questioned, sort of thrilled but still unsure. The officer then said, "Yes, sir, what seems to be the problem and where are you going?" I went into the politest, most obsequious delivery I could, responding, "I have driven all night, moving my belongings from South Texas to Austin to attend school. I am tired, yes, but I had no idea I was weaving." He then asked, "Do you have any contraband on you?" I thought to myself, "you have no fucking idea, at least not yet." I again said as politely as possible, "Uh, no, sir, not right on hand." He still had my driver's license and unbelievably said to me, "Well, son, at least you're honest." He then handed my license back and said, "Please be more careful and drive safely. Good day to you." Are you fucking kidding? I am blessed! Motherfucker, motherfucker, motherfucker! I pulled away, half a fucking million dollars richer.

There were actually many such scenarios, each as scary as the last. I trucked this contraband to the States alone for years. These were crazy times, but I loved this shit. In Port Isabel, I had made friends with a few of the local surfers and a handful of other ne'er-do-well residents. It was the crowd I was comfortable hanging with, and it kept me under the radar. We were all hippies, so I was well received. There was one particular couple I liked, Tom and Sandy. He was a surfer and she worked as a waitress in one of the local haunts. They were always looking for cash and I was able to facilitate their quest. They had a small rented house on the island where I was welcome to hang and stash my loads from San Benito before traveling through the Sarita checkpoint.

Eventually, I started renting U-Haul moving trucks because it didn't seem safe anymore driving it through in my Dream

Machine. Of course, none of it was safe. It just seemed to me that something had to be safer than the fucking Dodge routine. "Oh, yeah, baby, this will fool 'em!" Crazy enough, it did. I would load the weed, then proceed to load Tom and Sandy's entire household: washer/dryer, refrigerator, couches, beds, any and all furniture that would fit and obscure the weed. The border patrol agents were going to have to unload a ton of shit, if they thought there might be a load of weed behind it. I can assure you they would have in a heartbeat had there been any suspicion. I would don a wig and pin my long hair underneath, trim my mustache, and change my clothing to that of a truck driver. Again, I was feeling mighty clever. This was stupid, reckless, and risky fucking shit, but I made it through on multiple occasions. Like I said, I had stupid luck. I moved Tom and Sandy's household back and forth from Austin to the Valley countless times. From what I read in the paper, the Mexicans are continuing to use this same technique, though with marginal success.

Eventually, another student in Cholula approached me about getting involved in my smuggling enterprise. His name was Scott. He was a fiery redheaded, bearded, long, tall Texan, a great dude. Scott and I had gone from grade school through high school together in San Antonio, and coincidentally now found ourselves attending the same college, deep in Mexico. How the hell did that ever happen? He was from the same drug-drenched background as I, and all of this held nothing but intrigue for both of us. Scott actually became my first partner in my illicit business scheme.

Scott lived in a large and very old hacienda on the outskirts of Cholula, a badass place that he shared with a few other students. My ranch at the base of Popo (short for Popocatepetl) was only a few miles from Scott. One day, he was coming into town from his hacienda and I, at the same moment, was returning from town on one of my motorcycles. These were dirt roads and usually had very little traffic, maybe only a burro pulling a cart. Fuck, I could shoot past that like a bolt of lightning. I was hauling ass as I approached a blind corner, and believed I was going so fast there was not a chance anybody could hit me. Unfortunately, I was mistaken. Suddenly, this three-quarter-ton cattle-guarded front-bumpered Ford truck T-boned me in the middle of the intersection.

Unbelievably, it was fucking Scott! This motherfucker knocked me thirty feet in the air and left me mangled in a pile of dust in less than a second. Scott jumped out of his truck and came running over, just knowing he had killed me. He was horrified and screamed, "My god, Sandy, are you alright, motherfucker?" There was still a large cloud of dust surrounding me in the air. It was the dry season in Cholula and dirt roads were *puro pulvo*. I was stunned and unable to talk as the breath was completely knocked out of me. He was freaking out! "Dude, talk to me, are you OK?" I shook my head and spit the dust from my mouth as I tried to answer him, "I don't know yet." He was thrilled to hear any words I could utter. He pulled the motorcycle off me and helped me up. "Fuck, dude, let's get you to a hospital!" "Nah, just help me to your truck and take me home," I said to him through my painful and labored breath. I was definitely hurt, but still all in one piece and just wanting to get to the ranch and lie down. I would try and figure out what to do from there. Turned out I only had a few bruised ribs and a fractured wrist, but honestly, I was lucky to be alive. Apparently, I am a survivor.

As I said, I was more than happy to gain Scott as a partner. We were both from San Antonio, there was complete camaraderie, and he loved the idea of smuggling as much as I did. It was totally captivating! There was nothing like serving the Cause;

however, there was a mild initiation fee Scott had to pay in order to team up with me. I required that he ride up into the mountains of Oaxaca and make the treacherous exchange of money for weed with the peasant farmers. As previously described, this was some scary shit, so I welcomed his assistance. I will never forget his first night. I waited at the bottom of the hill in my truck while he ascended the dark, mountainous path. Hours later, he came roaring back down in the middle of the night, eyes wide as fucking full moons, with the back of his camper and tailgate bound together with twine to hold in the overflowing bounty of weed. It was a scary initiation for Scott, but it allowed me to avoid this same risk I'd previously taken alone. Unfortunately for Scott, this became one of his primary assignments. Scott had now qualified as a member of the club.

That was not the end of it. Next, we had a four-hour, mountainous drive from Oaxaca back to Cholula, still in the middle of the night. There was sunrise to worry about, as weed was falling out of the back of his truck, and there were, also, arbitrary military checkpoints to avoid. So zipping along at a high rate of speed was essential. Scott and I used CB radios to communicate between our two trucks. The lead truck or "front door" would stay a couple of miles ahead, just to identify any issues that might compromise our stealthy progression. These included police or military checkpoints, roadblocks, turned over trucks, etc. The radios were fairly sophisticated devices for this particular time period and especially for this far south of the border. They also worked well for our movements once we hit the States.

As we arrived back in Cholula from our all-night adventure, we would quickly maneuver through the back roads to the ranch and unload our weed. A huge sense of relief and excitement would wash over us as we emptied the trucks and readied ourselves for food, rest, and perhaps even a college class or two. Hey, we still had school to attend. *Dios mios*, it was crazy.

As the weeks rolled by, Scott and I would meet back at the ranch and begin to package and transfer the large burlap bales of weed into plastic garbage bags for the transport to the states. Rolls and rolls of duct tape were used to compact and secure the weed in the bags. We would ready our vehicles as well, tuning the trucks and airing the tires. It was a hell of a ride in front of us, and we were hoping for no breakdowns. The journey was close to a thousand-mile drive with lots of treacherous spots along the way. One in particular was an antiquated, rope-pulled barge used to cross a small river shortly before reaching Tampico, which was approximately halfway to the border from Cholula. There were also a couple of fueling stops along the way, which left us extremely vulnerable.

The trucks were packed with our bales of weed, from top to bottom, back to front. You never knew when you might pass a parade of military vehicles convoying along with the soldiers glancing your way. I remember when one of the weed-filled trucks broke down, and I had to use a couple of Oaxacan hammocks planned as family gifts for tow ropes just to keep the brigade moving north. Whatever it took, we needed to keep the trucks on the blacktop moving forward to the border.

At school, Scott and I went about our daily routines, keeping our secret to ourselves. We could not boast about something of this magnitude, even though most of our classmates probably indulged in smoking some grass. During this period, drugs were still part of the student culture, even in Cholula. Everybody seemed to be experimenting with everything: mushrooms, LSD, pills, and lots of grass. Cocaine was not yet popular. It was still peace and love and the rock revolution.

There was a group of Mexican artisans that came to the university every Thursday. They sat on the lawn and sold their wares: jewelry, blankets, and clothes. One in particular sold pottery and beads, as well as magic mushrooms. So for a weekend folly, you could purchase a couple of small bags of mushrooms along with your curios right on campus. Crazy.

At one point during these industrious times, my childhood friend Alf came down to visit me. I had promised his mom I wouldn't let him get into any trouble. Are you fucking kidding me? Trouble was my middle name. Alf arrived at the ranch, and I immediately threw him into my truck and sped off toward Oaxaca with Scott trailing behind me in his truck. We were taking money down to Ricardo and Boch to set up for another load. Oh yeah, Alf wouldn't be in any trouble. After the adventurous mountain trip, with Scott and me using our CB radios to pass numerous vehicles at a time on dangerously blind curves, Alf was starting to enjoy himself. Trouble? We were just getting started.

Four hours later, we arrived in Oaxaca safely, much to Alf's surprise. However, he was having a blast by now, and I was more than happy to oblige. We met up with Boch and Ricardo and took care of our business. Then we all decided we would head over to Puerto Angel for a few days of fun in the sun. The trip to Puerto Angel was always far more treacherous than the trip from Cholula to Oaxaca. There were dirt and mountainous roads the whole way, eight hours more of them to be exact. Of course, we were smoking multiple joints between the tequila and beer we consumed in mass quantities all along the way. However, this time we had a convoy of three trucks, each one trying to outpace the other. I felt confident that Alf was never in any danger, just as I had promised his mom.

We arrived safely, as usual, because this was the usual way we traveled, fucked up and at high speeds. Ricardo and Boch headed over to Ricardo's house, and Scott, Alf, and I went to secure hotel rooms close to the beach. I was attempting to show Alf the time of his life and so far so good. The little hotel we checked into was charming and just a short walk to the beach. Puerto Angel was very cool as it sat on the Pacific Ocean with its deep blue water and beautiful beaches. It was a great getaway if you had the means to get there.

While we were beaching it and strolling back and forth to our hotel, we met an older French woman with her son and his ex-girlfriend. Oh, everybody was goo-goo for this girl, whereas I was somewhat indifferent. Too much competition for my liking, and she was strutting around like some prima ballerina. I paid her little attention. The mother, however, was extremely friendly and approachable. She happened to be a flight attendant for Air France. We sat on the beach together and conversed back and forth about the usual things while getting to know each other. At one point, she asked me in her charming French accent, "So whoot doo you doo?" For the first time in my life, I decided to tell the truth and responded, "I'm an international drug smuggler." As unconcerned and casual as if I had said real estate broker, she replied in her beautifully accented English, "Ooo…zat zounds like a wreally goood zjob." I kind of looked at her with an air of surprise and said, "Well, yes, not so bad. Pays the bills."

We spent the next few days at the beach together while my buddies were falling all over themselves for the little, pretentious, French ballerina. I could have cared less. A few days into our trip, we invited our new French friends to join us for a little party. We decided to buy some fish and create somewhat of a fiesta. The French woman made homemade mayonnaise for the event. I had always hated mayonnaise, but this chick was French and insisted I try it, as it had French origins. Well, I was totally caught by surprise; the mayonnaise was exquisite, blended egg whites and lemon, who knew? (What's up, Hellman's?)

I was having a great time interacting with this woman and informed her, "Hey, we are getting ready to head back to my ranch in Puebla. Would you like to come along?" What the fuck? This was the way we rolled, anyone and everyone was always welcome. She gracefully accepted. However, her son and his ballerina girlfriend returned to France. Right on, baby, let's hit it!

We fired up the convoy, CB radios and all, and headed to the ranch. Alf was sitting passenger with the Air France attendant between us, and Scott was in the lead. We always made it exciting, simply because it was, hauling ass through the mountains and in our convoy. We pulled into the ranch at a high rate of speed and subsequently skidded to a halt at my large front doors. Goddamn, it was hard not to be impressed with ourselves. Motherfucker, we just knew we had to be some bad mofos.

I had an entourage of people staying at the ranch: the two girls, now Alf, and a few additional hangers-on. I offered the French woman her own room and whatever amenities she may have required. After a few days, we were all sitting around the living room with a fire blazing in the fireplace, smoking joint after joint, when the French woman entered and asked if anyone would like a massage. Everybody present was somewhat dumbfounded at the offer and hesitated out of a weed-induced stupor, so I said, "Why sure," only trying to be accommodating.

We retreated to my room and she asked that I disrobe for my "massage." I was clueless about what would happen next. This woman started doing things to me I never expected in my wildest dreams. I had thought myself to be quite the cocksman, however, this self-label was apparently supported by little, and ultimately showed itself to be a complete and utter misnomer. I was a rag doll in the hands of this woman. Oh, my god, she did things to me, apparently very French, that I had never imagined. I was only twenty-three, and completely unprepared for the extent of what I experienced sexually. Motherfucker, I still tingled the next day! Wow! I had made a new discovery…I loved the French!

The next day Alf and the French woman left around the same time for Mexico City to board their flights back to their designated homelands. In retrospect, I think that each of us enjoyed the time of our lives during those previous sun-filled days. At least for me, I'll never forget that time we spent together. I was so glad Alf came.

CHAPTER FIVE

Won't you roll me easy, oh so slow and easy
Take my independence, with no apprehension, no tension
You're a walkin', talkin' paradise, sweet paradise

… "Roll Um Easy" by Lowell George

Scott and I were crossing the border multiple times during this period. We had to have something to give us a reason for so many crossings. Antiques and pottery, therefore, became our guise. We were amateur importers as well as students. We hoped that would be sufficient because the border agents were becoming more curious, and at each passing there was now a record. Once they asked for our driver's licenses, our entire history of entry and reentry was spit out on their computers. There was no faking it.

I had once been caught with a quarter pound of weed in my door panel back in the days when I attended college in Austin. The agents brought out the dogs and, subsequently, found the weed and impounded my car. Thankfully, that's all they did, so no arrest record. However, the data of the find was still placed on my record with customs. This incident came up whenever I was crossing back into the States, so I was always scrutinized when entering—common practice.

During Christmas break 1975, at age twenty-four, I was returning home to spend the holiday with my family. I decided to leave my truck in Cholula and take a flight to the border. I had been eating Hycodan for some time and had acquired a bit of an addiction. I didn't want to be without them over the duration of my stay, so I loaded three hundred to four hundred pills into a small jar and stuck it in my boot. Again, I had to give this careful thought to ensure that I could get them through customs. I had it: I would fly to Matamoros and take a cab across. With hundreds of pills in my boot, I arrived at the airport and jumped into a cab. At the border, the agent in charge stopped the cab and requested my driver's license. He entered my license number into their database and asked that I step out of the cab and follow him. *Uh oh, I'm fucked!* I quickly assessed my predicament and decided immediately that I had only one choice: take the offensive.

He was escorting me inside to do a strip search when I stopped in my tracks and said, "Look, I've had just about my fill of the harassment I have had to endure every time I cross the border. I'm a student at the University of the Americas in Mexico, and I must cross the border multiple times during the school year. In addition, I have been strip-searched on countless occasions and continue to pass your scrutiny. In fact, I was just stripped-searched the previous time I crossed and I am fucking sick of this shit! I understand I have a small marijuana incident that pops up on your report, but that was years ago and I am goddamned sick and tired of being harassed continually for an error in judgment made back when I was only a kid. I am a student in Mexico, I learned my lesson years ago, and plain and simple, I refuse to continue to tolerate this style of harassment!" I was quivering in my loaded boots waiting on his response, yet tried for a face of innocence and the demeanor of an irate church lady. Motherfucker, this was not dress rehearsal.

The agent turned and stared at me authoritatively, then said, "OK, son, get out of here and have a nice day." Oh my fucking god! I wanted to kiss him. I had done it again. I stepped back into the cab, closed the door, and stretched out my arms and legs, settling into the backseat as it sped away. I pulled the bottle of Hycodan out of my boot and consumed a sizable handful of pills in celebration of my most recent victory. Jesus, was I ever lucky!

The next Christmas Eve, Scott dropped a load of weed off with the Mexicans on the Mexican side of the border and drove to Laredo to help divert any attention from crossing in Matamoros so often. He was loaded with a truck full of pottery and planned to pick up the weed later from the Mexicans. When he arrived at the American side, he was stopped by the border patrol agents, who requested he empty his truck of all merchandise and submit a declaration of the entire contents. Scott was trying to get home to celebrate the Christmas holiday with his family. Time was precious, and Scott was not in the mood for border hassle. One agent in particular really started fucking with him. He made Scott leave his truck overnight, so they could scrutinize the contents. I repeat: it was Christmas fucking Eve! Scott rented a hotel room on the American side and came back the next day to retrieve his truck. As he was loading all the pottery, the same border patrol agent continued to harass him as border patrol agents usually do.

Before he put one of the last pieces into the rear of his truck, Scott took one large ceramic burro with a basket on each side and threw it at the agent's feet. It was one big heavy piece of pottery and broke into a million pieces. The agent cried out, "You pick that up, and now!" Scott, in return, said to the agent, "Fuck you and Merry Christmas, asshole. That's your motherfucking Christmas present from me to you!" Then he casually got into the driver's seat of his truck and drove away. That must have gone over well…but that was not the end of it.

A year later, Scott and I were crossing at Matamoros together, this time with four macaws and a large white cockatoo. We had two red macaws as well as a green. They were all incredibly beautiful birds. Additionally, I had $20,000 stuffed in the frame of my truck under the rear window. I was nervous, to say the least. We declared all of the birds, but for one reason or another, Scott still had a recent receipt for the cockatoo in his wallet. Customs required that you had to own the birds for six months prior to crossing, and they had to be in your personal care for that length of time to be legal. We had forged all the necessary documents that reflected these requirements, but the receipt in Scott's wallet created some conflict. As a result, they kept all the birds as well as my truck overnight. I was real nervous at that point with the twenty g's hidden in the rear window frame. Incredibly, the border patrol agent in charge turned out to be the same one Scott had thrown the burro at a year earlier in Laredo. We were fucked!

We returned from our hotel room on the American side the next day to retrieve my truck and our cargo. Unbelievably, they didn't find my $20,000. We got all the birds back except for the cockatoo. Afterward, they followed us with unmarked cars north of the border for approximately a hundred miles, but motherfucker, we beat them again! We returned to pick up our load in San Benito a few days later, and "all was well!" Damn, I loved this shit!

I chose what I thought were subversive names for my two macaws to represent my endeavors. One was Sarita, in homage to the checkpoint, and the other Chichicapa, in honor of a small township in Oaxaca. Some of our truckloads came out of Chichicapa and some of our best weed. We moved high-quality weed. I am confident Scott and I introduced the first *colas* ever seen in Texas, if not in the whole United States. *Cola* means "tail" in Spanish. The weed smuggled in before us came in tight little blocks; in fact, they were referred to as "bricks." So, most of the weed entering the United States came from these smashed weed bricks. Scott and I likened it to "shit weed." Our weed was long-stemmed, flowery, foot-long *colas*. It was beautiful stuff.

We got into the marketing of our weed as well. Our buyers always wanted to know, "what kind of weed is this?" Users and buyers alike had never seen this kind of weed. Therefore, Scott and I invented names for it. One we decided to call Chichicapa, an exotic and mystical name for some exotic and high-potent shit. Our marketing scheme went well. So well, in fact, that once when I was in New York somebody I had never met offered to roll a joint for me. He was crazy about his weed and confided in all seriousness, "It's called Chichicapa." Well, I almost fell out of my chair. Here I was in New York City and my marketing skills had traveled all this way. It was a very proud moment for me. I never alluded to the fact that I had smuggled the shit in and named it myself. Crazy!

The trucks kept moving from Oaxaca to Austin with a short stay at the border while our loads were crossed. The money was flowing and the good times, too. Unfortunately, there were also some bad times. Some of the players peeled off as various mishaps occurred involving lost loads, drivers, trucks, and money. David (aka Lightning Wes Carver) even ended up in jail. He got caught driving one of my loads north and spent a year or more in a Mexican prison outside of Tampico. I tried to take good care of him throughout his imprisonment. I hired attorneys to help get him out and sent him cash to make his stay more comfortable. I made lots of visits to see him as well. David's "cell" was a small, metal-partitioned, private room with no bars or windows. Incredibly, I was able to visit him in his room. He had a bed, several colorful Mexican blankets, a small radio, and various other simple comforts. We listened to music, chatted about life in general, and maybe drank a beer or two. Money bought anything in there…except freedom. David maintained his sense of humor throughout. During one visit close to his release, he informed me that he had grown so fond of his surroundings, he was planning to buy a "Dempster Dumpster" to live in after he got out. He was a funny fuck.

Before David was shanghaied and stuck in the Tampico prison, we were still attending our classes and playing night after night at the bars in Cholula. We were even invited to play at a talent show put on by the university. There was a sell-out crowd and we put on our best show ever. It was so thrilling to stand on stage in front of our peers with a packed house and raving applause. We brought the house down.

We gained a bit of notoriety that night, but there was one more element that made the evening particularly special. While backstage with the other participants in the show, I fell in love with a ballerina. She was the most beautiful girl I'd ever seen. It just so happened this was the same gorgeous Asian girl I had noticed my first day on campus. Between our performances, we were sitting on the floor backstage watching the other acts when she started playing footsy with me. I was taken by surprise. I had admired her from afar for some time, but I was convinced there would be no way she would ever find anything remotely attractive about me, let alone allow me to capture her heart. I was a drug-crazed, smuggling, guitar-playing cowboy, and she was a goddess.

Jennifer was her name, and she would soon become my Maid Marian. She had long, black silky hair down to the middle of her back—hair like I had never seen before. Her Asian genetics were something I was unfamiliar with, and I was quite infatuated. She was graceful and sure of herself and undeniably an iconic beauty. I will never forget that night.

Months went by before our courtship blossomed. I was afraid to move too quickly because I didn't want to appear a complete doofus. I did quit smoking weed altogether, since I knew she was not a pot smoker. Hell, I was in love! I did not quit my smuggling, however, as I was in love with that as well. During my supposed courtship, Scott and I made another run to the border and were gone for about a month. When I returned to the ranch, I asked the girls if either of them had seen or heard from Jennifer. They said they thought she had a new boyfriend. "No fucking way!" I proclaimed, and asked if they knew where he lived. They did. This was a small college town and most everyone was aware of everybody else's business. I was devastated but wasn't going to let that motherfucker get in my way.

I ran to my room and collected a Rod Stewart song I had previously written down in longhand on notebook paper, folded it, and shoved it in my pocket. The song was "Every Picture Tells a Story." At the bottom of the song, I had written: "To Jennifer, from Sandy." I was trying to make it appear as if I had written this song for her. Plagiarism was the least of my worries; I was at risk of losing my girl! With song in hand, I jumped on one of my dirt bikes and sped off directly toward the new boyfriend's house. I was hauling ass, weaving through the streets of Cholula, bound and determined I was going to fight for my Maid Marian! I came screaming and sliding to a stop on my noisy motorcycle, jumped off, and made a confident knock upon his door.

The door opened, and there stood What's His Name with Jennifer behind him. They were apparently having a little dinner party. Courtesies were exchanged, during which he kept eyeing and admiring my bike. It suddenly occurred to me I could take advantage of his interest and be alone with Jennifer. I told him, "Dude, try it on for size. Take it for a ride!" Little did he know I was in the process of taking him for a ride.

He jumped on my bike with enthusiasm and sped off down the street. As Jennifer and I stood and watched him speed off, I turned to her and stated, "So, I hear this is your new boyfriend. What's that all about?" Jennifer shrugged her shoulders and said, "I don't know," and looked at me in a questioning manner. I said, "That's some bullshit, are you kidding me?" She looked back at me and smiled, not saying anything. It was then I apologized for being gone so long, handed her the folded paper, and said, "Here, this is a song I wrote for you." She smiled up at me, slowly slipped the paper into the pocket of her jeans, and kissed me softly on the lips. I was convinced Maid Marian was now mine.

What's His Name came speeding back on my bike, utterly exuberant with delight, thanking me again and again for the experience he had just had. I, on other hand, thanked him as well with the same, if not more, magnified exuberance. I had just slain my opponent, as Robin Hood had done on so many Saturday mornings in Sherwood Forest. We said our good-byes and I jumped back on my bike, fired it up, and sped off into the sunset.

Jennifer was never of the criminal sort; in fact, she had never even smoked grass. She was a bright young college student and assuredly naïve to my secret life. However, she had to have recognized the outlaw in me because that was hard to disguise... but what beautiful maiden doesn't fall for a bad boy? I was a big fish in a little pond. I played in a band, drove motorcycles, lived on a big ranch, and had lots of money. I took Jennifer on many exciting trips to the Caribbean and other exotic resorts. We traveled the heck out of Mexico and always made it a whirlwind tour. However, even though extravagant, we tried to maintain somewhat of a low profile; in fact, the lower the better. Flash was a little dangerous in our business; only the money mattered.

One trip we took was to Puerto Angel. It had a small airport with a grass strip that accommodated small commercial airplanes. Jennifer and I, along with Scott and his date, flew in on one of them. Once we landed and disembarked, the *Federales* approached us with waving hands and said, "No, no, no *señor*... this way, this way, we want to get a photo of you," herding us away from the other passengers, suitcases in hand. We went willingly, assuming we were all so glamorous that they wanted to use our photo for a travel brochure. There we stood, arms around each other, mugging for the camera. Only later did we realize they were tracking our fucking asses!

At this point in time, university classes were disrupted from a strike the teachers had formed trying to unionize their group. The Mexican college would have nothing to do with that. It was a stalemate between administration and teachers with no end in sight. Many of us stayed, but the crowd was starting to thin out. Scott and I decided to move our operation to Austin but keep a place in Cholula as well. Jennifer saddled up with us and followed me back to Texas. Apparently, she found my lifestyle very alluring.

CHAPTER SIX

*I read the papers
And I got the blues
I'm so sad to hear the news
Help wanted, but not enough
You know these times are gettin' rough*

... *"Long Distance Love" by Lowell George*

By June 1976, the operations hub had moved from Cholula to Austin. Jennifer and I rented a small bungalow where we lived for about a year. In addition, we maintained a house in Cholula that served as our Mexican headquarters. We would stay there for months at a time. It wasn't long before one of our drivers flipped Scott's truck close to the border and lost the load. Bales of weed were strewn all over the highway and Scott's truck ended up on its side. He had to leave it behind and haul ass to the border. With Scott's truck in the hands of the Mexican authorities, he was fearful of repercussions and decided to get out of the business. This left me primarily alone until I hired additional drivers.

It soon became obvious to me that we needed to start flying the loads out. The border was tightening up along with the checkpoints. This was happening in both Mexico and Texas. It was growing more and more difficult with the expanded use of drug-sniffing dogs and the heightened awareness of the border agents.

Trucking it to the states, therefore, turned to flying it in, but there was still the exercise of getting it out of the mountains of Oaxaca. This required that our trucks move the weed to a secret landing strip in Mexico where we would store it until we could fly back to pick it up. There was a considerable amount of travel involved. I was making thousand-mile trips each way from Austin, to Cholula, to Oaxaca and back, alone in the cab of my truck. To make the trip more enjoyable, I had the most hopped-up stereo and speakers money could buy. My closest traveling companions became Bonnie Raitt, Linda Ronstadt, and Little Feat, who took center stage. They were "the best unknown rock band" ever. I was completely blown away with the lead vocals and slide guitar of Lowell George as well as his song writing. He was undeniably the catalyst for the band's success. I barreled down the road for hours, even days at a time, with their music blaring through my speakers. Turn it up, motherfucker!

As mentioned, CB radios were extremely critical to our smuggling business and responsible for our survival in Mexico. They had become popular along the US highways as well. All CB operators had to have a call sign and I had chosen "Sailin' Shoes" as mine, a name I had ripped from a Lowell George tune, "Put on your Sailin' Shoes." One night, I was leaving Austin on my way back to Cholula. Suddenly, a guy came back at me, "By chance, Sailin' Shoes isn't a reference to Little Feat, is it?" "Well, hell yes it is!" I responded, shocked by this guy's recognition. "Have you got their new album?" he asked. Turned out he was the representative for Warner Brothers Records and asked me if I wanted a copy. We met on the side of the road shortly thereafter and he handed me their newest release free of charge. Cosmic intervention is all I can say about that. (I was sad to learn that Lowell George died two years later from a drug overdose in June of 1979.)

Since my range of travel had become so extensive, it had also impacted my personal life. In June of 1977, my sister was getting married in New York City. I was concluding a deal in Oaxaca, Mexico, at that time and had to drive thirty hours straight back to Austin in order to pick up Jennifer, and then drive back to San Antonio to catch a flight to New York City. Motherfucker, it was exhausting, but the prenuptial events were scheduled for the next day. It was crazy. I had been in Oaxaca the morning before and suddenly found myself in New York City, sick with fatigue.

According to my sister, I created quite a spectacle when I showed up at the stately rehearsal dinner dressed in a tuxedo with shoulder-length hair, elephant-skin boots, and an exotic Asian on my arm. "New York had never seen anything like it," my brother-in law laughed. My sister's conservative friends whispered to her in confidence, "Who is this guy?" "Oh…that's my brother," she confessed. I always left her a little uneasy, as we moved in different worlds. She was a thirty-year-old successful Wall Street statistician working for New York's Special Narcotics' Court and marrying an East Coast attorney, whereas I was a twenty-five-year-old drug-smuggling millionaire renegade motherfucker. This always seemed to create a little conflict.

Back in Austin, there were nights I was notified that a load of weed was coming in from Mexico. I would tell Jennifer I needed to go "catch a plane" (i.e., meet it on a dark vacant road outside of town) and sometimes invited her to go along. We would wait in the dark until alerted by a two-way radio, and then I would turn on my headlights and hold a spotlight out my driver's side window to help indicate where we were. The plane would be upon us before we knew it. I would then point the spotlight and the headlights down the dirt road in front of us, lighting its way. The plane would come in over the cab of my truck and land ahead of us. I would immediately drive down to where it had stopped, unload it with the boys, and transfer the load to my truck. It was a simple procedure. I shouldn't imply that it was commonplace, but it was. We almost forgot it was illegal. Jennifer and I became very casual about the whole affair as we traveled to Oaxaca, Mexico City, border towns, and across the country, buying and selling my weed. It was business as usual.

One of the best connections I had for selling my loads was a guy named Billy in Albuquerque, New Mexico. I would either truck my weed to him in New Mexico, or he would come pick it up in Austin with his own vehicles and drivers. We made a ton of money together. This dude could move thousands of pounds of weed at a time and always paid cash. As far as buyers were concerned, Billy was the king. During one of our deals, I rode around New Mexico with him. He was carrying about $50,000 in cash, separated into individual envelopes containing $10,000 each. We drove from one town to the next as he paid off state officials for something I never quite understood. I was just along for the ride and thought this exercise of his was probably none of my fucking business.

One night, I was alone in Albuquerque picking up some cash from Billy for a load of weed, and he said, "Hey, man, Willie Nelson is in town playing tonight, and he happens to be a good friend of mine. You want to go to the concert?" "Well, sure," I replied, "Fuckin' A." I had heard from so many people on so many occasions that Willie Nelson "is a good friend of mine"; I simply took it with a grain of salt. Billy called the club where Willie was playing and discovered it was a sold out performance. He turned to me and said, "Don't sweat it; we'll get in." I was thinking the whole time, "Yeah, right," but I didn't want to offend my million-dollar man and agreed, "Let's get the fuck out of here and go see him!"

We arrived at the club around ten that night. There was a line of about a hundred people curved around the block, all waiting to get in. I was thinking once again, "No fucking way, dude; we don't stand a chance." Billy looked at me and said, "Let me check the back door, OK?" Well hell, I was down with that. Billy proceeded to "pound, pound, pound" on the back door until it finally opened. There stood one of the roadies for Willie, who hollered out, "Billy, you motherfucker, what the fuck is happening?" I was totally caught by surprise. Billy introduced me and asked the guy, "Can you get us in?" "Well, hell yes, motherfuckers, come on in!" Next thing I knew, Willie was shaking my hand and embracing Billy. "Y'all stick around and enjoy the show. Eat all you can here backstage. Can I buy y'all some drinks?" Willie asked cordially. Well, fuck me running. I met all the band members that night, drank till I was stupid, and saw the best up-close Willie Nelson concert I'd ever seen. In fact, I drank so many free "lemon drops" that night, I have never ordered one since. Billy was a bad motherfucker.

That was not the only celebrity connection Billy had in the world of sex, drugs and rock 'n' roll, and the more business we did together, the more adventures unfolded. Billy later asked me to meet him in LA to retrieve some of the cash he owed me. I hopped on a flight from Austin to LAX, arriving in Los

Angeles a few hours later. Los Angeles was unfamiliar territory for me at this point in my life, but apparently not for Billy.

He picked me up at the airport and the next thing I knew I was walking into a small apartment in Malibu. Where we were I hadn't a clue, but Billy said he was taking me to see some friends. I became a little starry-eyed, as I passed through a hallway on the way back to someone's bedroom. Each side of the hallway was adorned with gold record albums and photos with salutations. One said, "To Jesse, my prodigal son, love John Lennon." There was another gold album indicating, "With love to my brother," signed George Harrison. Motherfucker, there were multiple ones from Rod Stewart and another from Jackson Brown, Taj Mahal, Leon Russell, Bob Dylan, and on and on. I was totally blown away. When I arrived at the bedroom, there was the guitarist, Jesse Ed Davis, sitting cross-legged on his king-size bed with a couple of his cronies stretched out around him. They were just shooting the breeze and hanging out with a dinner plate positioned between them containing a big pile of white powder.

I was introduced to the crowd in the bedroom and said to Jesse, "Goddamn, dude, that's quite an impressive hallway you've got there." Jesse looked at me appreciatively and stated, "Oh, yeah, I refer to that as my Wall of Shame." Motherfucker, there must have been twenty gold albums and photos from the biggest names ever in rock 'n' roll history. Jesse had played lead on Jackson Brown's "Doctor My Eyes" and told me he had recently been kicked off tour with Rod Stewart for heroin abuse. Who would have ever thought you could get terminated from a rock band for drug abuse? Fucking crazy!

I gratefully exchanged pleasantries and was trying to look as cool as I could when Jesse said to me, "Would you like some?" referring to the white powdery substance in front of him. What the fuck was I supposed to say? I replied, "Well, hell yes, let's get the party started!" It was only three in the afternoon, but wasn't I sort of on vacation? I was in LA goddammit, hanging with fucking rock stars! I decided to shake off my business frame of mind and relax. I took a big snort and waited for its effects. "Great coke, eh, Jesse?" "Oh, no, Sandy," Jesse replied, "That was some badass 'china white' heroin." Uh oh, I guess I should have asked that question a tad earlier. It wasn't as if I was unfamiliar with it; I just didn't think I was ready to relax quite so severely. I was about to be mighty fucked up. Parenthetically, Jesse Ed Davis died in 1988 after collapsing in a laundromat in Malibu, California, from an overdose of heroin. Good thing I didn't stick around any longer than I did.

Billy and I left Jesse Ed's place and headed to Dick Clark's old house in Malibu. I was not ready for this either. Billy was dating a sixteen-year-old girl, whose parents were residing in Dick's house overlooking the Pacific. I had no idea of their connection, but there I stood in a living room walled with plate-glass windows, looking down on Malibu Beach. There were even mirrors on the ceiling in the bedroom. Incredibly, the parents of Billy's adolescent interest were smoking PCP as I was introduced to them. Were they fucking kidding? This was some crazy shit. Oh, my fucking god, this was way too Californian for my conservative Texan upbringing. Regardless of my dope smoking, drug smuggling, and crazy background, these people had taken it to a whole new level. I declined to partake of their PCP offering. Sure, I had just done some heroin with Jesse Ed Davis, but fuck, I had to draw the line somewhere! (?) For god's sake, I was on a business trip.

Billy and I, with his teenager in tow, then headed into LA to do some partying, or should I say, more partying. Fuck, I was in bad shape from the smack by then. We went to the Roxy Theater along 77 Sunset Strip, probably one of the most famous clubs of that era. Everybody knew the Roxy, and I was real excited to be going, regardless of the fact that I could hardly keep my eyes open or my chin up off my chest. The heroin was also starting to upset my stomach. We made it to the Roxy, but I remember very little except stumbling out the back door and puking profusely in the alley. I don't believe we stayed much longer. Ah, but what fond memories of my night at the Roxy. I did survive the night's indulgences, however, and flew back home the next day $400,000 dollars richer, all the $100 bills stuffed into my leather briefcase and carry-on. It wasn't such a bad trip after all; I fucking loved California!

Once I got back to Austin, I decided I needed to buy a house. It was 1977 and I was twenty-five years old. I found an A-frame on Lake Austin located thirty miles outside of town at the bottom of Mansfield Dam. There was an additional fifteen to twenty minute drive down Steiner Ranch Road to get there. It was in the middle of nowhere—my kind of place. I was so full of myself, I didn't let Jennifer move in with me initially; "cause I needed my space." Apparently, I was just more in love with myself. She was heartbroken, and I knew I had fucked up big time. I seemed to be exceptionally good at creating resentment. There were some indiscretions on both sides as a result. However, I finally realized what I had lost and asked her to please come home.

Boch was frequently in Austin and always stayed with Jennifer and me at the lake house. As mentioned, it was extremely rural, just the way I liked it—outlaw territory. One morning, Boch went for a jog with our new eight-month-old Golden Retriever. Boch named him Zlato, which means "gold" in Bulgarian. Boch could be very clever at times. Unfortunately, he returned to the house from his jog and said he thought Zlato had been shot. He heard shots ring out and saw Zlato suddenly charging past him towards the woods. I got my shoes and followed Boch to where he thought Zlato had gone. Sure enough, there lay Zlato, dead under a brushy cedar tree. Fuck, I loved that dog and was really pissed off—in fact, I was enraged.

We carried him back to the house and gave him an immediate burial. Then I hopped into my truck and sped off to find out what the hell had happened. We were in the goddamned country, and this kind of shit made zero sense to us. I pulled up to the house where Boch thought the incident had occurred. I rolled down my window and shouted at a guy standing on the deck, "Hey man, did you happen to shoot my dog this morning?" The guy shouted back, "I sure did! Your dog was after some chickens in my yard." I got out of my truck and stared up at the guy. "What the fuck were you thinking, motherfucker? My buddy and my dog were only out for a morning fucking run, asshole!" He replied, "I guess you don't know who I am. I'm the sheriff of these parts." I said, "I don't give a fuck who you are. I'm the fucking sheriff of Nottingham, motherfucker."

I told him what a piece of shit I thought he was, and this would not be the end of it. I then took my hand and pointed it at him in the form of a pistol and let my thumb down, like I had pulled the trigger. Then I calmly brought it back to my lips and blew the end of my extended finger, as if I were blowing smoke out of the barrel. I stared him directly in the eyes and said, "See ya soon, motherfucker." I then opened the door of my truck and got in, flipping him off, as I slowly pulled away. I turned to Boch and said with disdain, "Fuck that dude!"

Every day after this heartbreaking incident, I would pull up to his house and honk my horn, honk it till the motherfucker walked outside. I would, again, slowly roll down my window, point my hand in pistol fashion, and pull the trigger. I was loving this shit. He actually was a sheriff's deputy with squad car and uniform, but I didn't give a rat's ass. He was mine. I wore that motherfucker out with my persistent stops and honking.

There was a small convenience store up on Highway 620 that all of us from the neighborhood frequented because it was the only one available for miles. One day, I saw him shopping for supplies in the canned-food aisle. He was dressed in his uniform with his cop car idling outside. I signaled him from the opposite end of the isle, "Psst," and as he turned and looked back at me, I stood in military fashion with both hands clasped and slowly extended my arms, pointing my fake pistol at him, and pulled the trigger. I drew my arms back in slow motion and blew the imaginary smoke from my barrel. "Fuck you, asshole," I said loud enough for him to hear. He didn't move a muscle. This kind of behavior is generally unheard of, especially for a full-time smuggler and a complete and utter outlaw. Regardless, I was relentless with this loser. I didn't care—he had killed my dog.

After about a month of my dedicated harassment of this asshole, I got a summons to appear in court. Of course, it was the sheriff's deputy versus me. I couldn't wait to see how this shit was going to turn out. The day came for my court appearance, and there I stood before the judge with the deputy at my side. The judge asked, "What seems to be the problem?" The deputy then started to spew his rhetoric about how he shot my dog and why. He then told the part about me constantly confronting him with my finger pistol. The judge almost fell out of his chair when he heard this. He looked down at me from his high perch, with glasses down his nose, elbows on his desk, and said, "You have got to be kidding me. Have you really been doing this?" I boldly looked back at him and said, "You're goddamned right, your honor, and proud of it. Fuck this guy. He killed my dog for no reason other than self-gratification, and I am goddamned pissed off!" I then added, "This is my goddamned neighbor. We both live out in the county blocks from each other, and these actions of his were totally uncalled for. Additionally, I will continue my demonstration until I feel satisfied."

The judge reared back in his chair and said, "Whoa, whoa, whoa, I can easily see the two of you are headed for disaster." He stalled for a moment and then said, "I am putting a restraining order on both of you; neither one of you can come within a thousand feet of each other." He raised his outstretched hands toward me and said authoritatively, "Please…please, Mr. Stokes, quit doing what you have been doing. My lord, are you crazy?" I replied, "Only if you make me." After the restraining order was put in place, I could speed past that motherfucker in my truck at 90 miles an hour, and he would never even begin to acknowledge me. Fuck that guy! I was the fucking sheriff of Nottingham.

For the next couple of years, Boch and I continued to move loads north; some were flown out while others were still trucked. We would try to move the loads on holidays when the cops were busy. One Fourth of July, we were moving a load north from Oaxaca via truck. I was so excited I went out and bought an entire fireworks stand in preparation for our celebration. Unfortunately, the truck flipped and the drivers lost the load. Motherfucker, about this time there seemed to be a series of mishaps with our loads, and I lost a half million dollars each time. I was starting to feel the financial crunch since we were still living an extravagant lifestyle. The income from the weed business was always feast or famine, and I never learned how to adjust my spending habits accordingly.

Jennifer was not working, and I was becoming a little resentful that she was depending on me to support her when I could barely take care of myself. I still loved her, but at the same time, I couldn't maintain responsibility for her during the periods I was losing so much income. Additionally, I assumed she wanted to get married and I was panic-stricken at the thought of commitment. My parents had been in a tumultuous relationship, and there was no way I wanted a repeat of their disastrous union. Besides, I was twenty-seven years old and an outlaw. I didn't want to end the relationship, I just wanted her to establish greater independence and pursue her own career. She decided to go back home to California, so I drove her there. I then returned to the lake house and tried to get another load together. Eventually, I got back on top of my game and things were going well.

In the meantime, Jennifer was looking for work in California. She had received a degree in dance from the University of the Americas and so traveled to Las Vegas to audition for a dance troupe in a casino. She was subsequently hired as a showgirl for the Hotel San Juan Casino in Puerto Rico. Vegas showgirl… goddammit I was proud of her.

Jennifer moved to Puerto Rico in 1979. After getting established, she suggested I come live with her. Since I was a smuggler, I could operate out of just about any location, so I sold my lake house to a friend and moved to Puerto Rico to set up headquarters. Jennifer had found a fabulous high-rise apartment overlooking the bay of Isla Verde. It faced west and offered a panoramic view of incredible sunsets. I purchased a '71 Impala from an ex-patriot moving back to the States. I was one of the few on the island that had a car, as it was expensive to import them. Jennifer and I traveled the island in that car, sometimes taking girls from the dance troupe along.

My first night in San Juan, I attended one of her shows. She was very excited about having me there and had told all the showgirls I was coming. She had even secured a seat for me in the front row. As she came gliding out onto the stage, I thought, "Oh my fucking god." There she was in a feathered headdress, sequined bikini, and spiked heels, parading across the stage in a cheesy routine. Shit, I didn't know what to think. I mean, this was my goddamned girlfriend up on stage, and I didn't think I necessarily approved. In fact, I didn't approve.

I sat there in the front row with a big scowl on my face. I couldn't control it. Despite my unorthodox lifestyle, I had a very conservative Texas background, plus I had never seen a Las Vegas-style show. I tried to quickly assess the dynamics of the situation, but I just couldn't seem to come to grips with it. It was all so foreign to me, plus I was in a jealous rage.

After the show, she asked, "So, what did you think?" It was obvious to her and likely the entire dance crew what I thought. All you had to do was look at me; I was in the front fucking row. I was still pissed and couldn't say a word. She looked at me with composure and said, "Sandy, we all worked very hard at these routines and if you don't like it, I suggest you don't even come." It took me a while to process; however, I realized Jennifer had gained her independence. Eventually, I came to respect all of the girls in the troupe. These were working girls making their own way in the world.

For me, things were status quo. I was still deeply involved in setting up planeloads of weed and moving them to Texas. I rambled between Puerto Rico, Mexico, South America, and the States. I would stay in our Puerto Rican apartment for a couple of months at a time, then charge off to fix some component of a deal in chaos. Things were never precisely organized and, in fact, often in disarray. There was always something disastrous happening somewhere and the need for crisis intervention. Therefore, Puerto Rico became my respite. This is where I relaxed and took in the culture.

While in Puerto Rico, my Spanish became even better. They speak a weird dialect on the island. They drop the "s" and change the "r" to an "l." When I arrived, some local informed me of these changes. "Shit," I said to him, "I can't even do that in English. How the hell am I going to do that in Spanish?" Well, it didn't take long. Once again, the locals were curious as to where I was from. I seemed to be very convincing when I told them I was from Puerto Rico. One time, I boarded a plane for Miami and sat down next to an obviously Puerto Rican woman. She asked me where I was from, and I responded in Puerto Rican dialect, "*Aqui, en Puerto Rico.*" I then asked her, "Where are you from?" She replied, "New Jork," in her strong Puerto Rican accent. That was some funny fucking irony.

Wind surfing was a brand new sport at the time. From my high-rise apartment, I sometimes saw one lone guy out there and said to myself, "I need to learn to do that!" Initially, I was horrible. The winds were always gusting at thirty miles per hour, and I would get stuck off shore a mile or so, not knowing how to turn around. I would have to take down the sail, roll it up as best I could, and paddle that motherfucker all the way back to shore, pissed off the whole way. Eventually, I learned the nuances of the sport, and in the end, I whooped that sailboard into submission. It was quite rewarding to be twenty-eight years old and living my life on the beaches of Puerto Rico, windsurfing all day and having fun in the sun.

Over time, I got to know that lone fellow surfer. His name was Carl and he was a carnie. Carl was pock-faced with a beard and kind of scruffy looking. He worked the midways of two traveling carnivals with a show that featured "the largest rat in the world," which was actually nothing more than a nutria. The fascinating thing about this guy was that he lived in a half-million-dollar condo on the water in Puerto Rico six months out of the year.

Who would've thought a carnie would have that kind of money? I'll never forget going up to his beautiful place overlooking the ocean with a sunken living room, leather couches, and thick white carpeting. How strange. This dude was banking it and a fucking carnie!

My relationship with Jennifer was unraveling about this time; I just didn't know it. I was away from Puerto Rico frequently on deals, which probably created resentment. Again, I can only assume that she had wanted to get married. That is what normal people were supposed to do after college: get married, settle down, and have a family. However, I never brought the subject up. I still had serious fears about marriage. I was haunted by my dad's advice years earlier, "Don't marry for love; marry for money." I knew this came from a broken heart, as he had never recovered from the loss of my mom through divorce. I also knew about broken hearts and had made a commitment to myself never to have another. This had a huge impact on me and seemed to dictate my behavior. I realized I had become a womanizer—an admittedly pejorative term, but it seemed to fit. I knew Jennifer was the right girl for me, but I couldn't make the commitment. Anybody in his right mind would have married this girl in a heartbeat…but I was out of my mind.

About this time, I was probably becoming more attentive to the stewardesses on my international flights than I was to Jennifer. Consequently, there were affairs on both sides. I have to admit, I lived by a double standard, and generally speaking, it was always more about me than anybody else in my life. I was completely self-absorbed and a renegade, so caught up in the smuggling and the freedom it bought me. I was a cowboy, a rebel, and a narcissist and would not be controlled.

We had lived together for four years, but finally the drugs, money, and, mostly, ego took precedence. I have few regrets, but I must take ownership for this one. It was one of the saddest days of my life when I came home from a drug run on my twenty-ninth birthday and found a pair of brown men's loafers on my side of the bed. I had been sleeping with a stewardess in Miami the night before; I just never imagined Jennifer would have been doing the same. It broke my heart, but I could not contain my jealousy, so I packed my bags the next day and left Puerto Rico and Jennifer, eventually ending up in an even wilder, more decadent single life back in Austin.

CHAPTER SEVEN

Billy got so sad, dejected, put on his hat and start to run
Runnin' down the street yellin' at the top of his lungs
All I want in this life of mine is some good clean fun
All I want in this life and time is some hit and run

… *"Fat Man in the Bathtub" by Lowell George*

"Could it be any darker in here?" I shouted at Jeff above the roar of the twin engines. He yelled back, "No shit!" The wing lights, strobe lights, and transponder were all in the "off" position. The instrument panel lights were also extinguished to hide our presence while crossing into the US. The twin propeller Cessna and the cabin were therefore as black as the night in front of us. Jeff and I were alone in the cockpit, packed in like sardines by bales of weed, cruising back to Houston from Veracruz. Speeding along in the sky, approximately thirty miles from the border, we began to see the lights of Matamoros and Brownsville ahead. We started our descent from ten thousand feet down to, literally, the tops of the trees. It was a ridiculous and dangerous altitude, fifty feet above the ground and traveling at a speed of two hundred miles per hour. Our intention was to avoid any suspected radar. Motherfucker, we were keeping a close look through our windshield.

Soon, we were just feet above Matamoros, Mexico, with the US-Mexico bridge directly below. Looking down, I could almost see the expressions on the faces of people wearing cowboy hats and brightly colored ponchos as they walked casually across the international bridge, looking up as surprised to see us as we were them, even briefly as it was. Actually, they may not have been able to see us through the glare of the city lights, but I assure you, they definitely could hear us. We were roaring unmistakably just above their heads.

It was easy for us to see from the plane with the bridge and city lit up like a sports arena. Imagine seeing an explosion of lights and then blowing over the tops of them. There were car headlights, streetlights, and cantina signs of shimmering neon below. Life was going on underneath us while we zoomed just slightly above the trees, telephone poles, and highlines. The cockpit was relatively quiet except for the roar of the dual engines. The adrenaline was flowing but the mood between us was serious and attentive. Shit, man, it was going on.

We skimmed the border around ten at night. We would be skipping immigration and due process altogether; stopping to chat with border patrol agents was out of the question. We both hoped our plan to cross directly over the tops of Matamoros and Brownsville would help keep us undetectable. I had previously concluded that the most obvious becomes the unobvious, and we were putting my formula to the test. We were concentrating on the flying while waving *adios* to Brownsville pedestrians below. As we sped away from the lights, I leaned toward Jeff and murmured, "Damn it dude, I think we're OK. Let's keep her rollin'." Jeff turned toward me and replied with only a nod.

Once the lights of Brownsville had passed below and behind, we started our climb, returning to a few thousand feet for the safety of more altitude. We stayed on course, keeping a bead toward our target. Our level of anxiety was beginning to increase in anticipation of the landing ahead. We would be setting down on a small dirt crop-duster strip in the middle of the night.

We were heading to the landing strip we had used many times before. It was located in Nada outside of Houston, appropriately named *Nada,* which means "nothing" in Spanish. Nada had a population of about thirty, and plenty of dark and vacant dirt roads or crop-duster strips on which to land, one of which was our favorite. After our border crossing, we were about an hour and a half from the trucks waiting on the runway. Generally speaking, we waited on good weather, wanting a clear and star-filled night to ensure our visibility. As crazy as we were, safety was still an important ingredient when our lives were at stake.

We had ground crew waiting on the remote crop-duster strip with truck headlights blinking and a hand-held spotlight positioned. Two-way radios were also part of our strategy, but their range was far from satisfactory. As a result, I began to alert the crew from a few miles out, shouting into the radio, "Hey, man, we are getting close, please light up what you can." Once we got a little closer, again using the radio, I shouted, "We're looking, we're looking, do you see us?" In the still of the night, the crew began to hear the roar of the plane in the distance. "We've got you guys, we see you," the radio crackled back.

By that time, we had reignited the strobe and wing lights to help coincide our efforts to rendezvous. The ground crew flashed headlights and pointed a spotlight toward the stars in our direction, both seen easily on the dark terrain below, marking our destination. As we flipped the switch, the landing lights of our twin Cessna were immediately illuminated. We passed over the dirt strip and then looped around to set up for our approach. Next, the gear and flaps went down. As we powered in, the ground coming closer and closer, we hit the dirt road, gravel spraying, and bumped a few times before the nose wheel grabbed the ground. It was man versus metal. We were in a race for our lives to stop this motherfucker before we came to the end of the road and hit the cows standing in the plowed fields ahead.

Once on the ground, the night pierced by our roar, the goal was simple: keep it straight, as the big hunk of metal rolled fast and furious at one hundred-plus miles per hour, straddling ditches along both sides of our dirt runway. Still roaring, both engines thrusting, we rolled to a stop. The plane lights, headlights, spot, and propellers were then abruptly extinguished. It was time to jump out and rally the ground crew. Jordan hollered through the windshield, "You guys alright?" We both looked at him and presented our thumbs up. "We're OK!" we hollered back.

The crew rushed over, unloaded, and filled the awaiting van with the numerous bales stuffed in the back of the plane. All this was done as quickly and methodically as possible. Goddamned cowboys we were, high-fiving and slapping each other's backs at the success of the trip. "Yes, sir, boys, now let's get the fuck out of here," I yelled with zeal. At this point of the game, the adrenaline was high, real high, and we got out of there just as fast as we came in. As the trucks and crew were pulling away and heading into Houston, it was then in our hands to spin the plane around in pirouette fashion with engines fired back up.

We were feeding those twins all the fuel they could take to throttle us back down the dirt road and, subsequently, back into the night air. "Yeah, baby. *Adios*, motherfuckers!"

Exciting as it may sound, it was twice that—again a real-life cat-and-mouse game, and somehow we had gotten pretty good at it. Damn, it was exhilarating! We used the strip in Nada multiple times until the resident farmer got fairly hip to what was going on. His home sat on the property not more than a few hundred yards away. We were trespassing and poaching in the biggest way and making noisy fucking departures in the process. Eventually, after numerous notable landings, the roar of our plane must have alerted him, and he, apparently, telephoned the police. There they came—speeding down the dirt road toward us with lights flashing and sirens screaming. Baby, we had us a chase on. Luckily, with multiple vehicles going every which way and the plane taking off from a rice field in the middle of the night, we simply overwhelmed the small local police force. I thanked the universe for that one. After this incredible cosmic intervention, we never returned to try our luck in Nada. We chalked this place up to the history books. No more Nada, never again. Ah, but what a great run it was! We had to find a new location.

My co-pilot, Jeff, was a tall, thin, good-looking guy with blue eyes and olive skin, an incredible pilot, especially for someone of his age, in his mid-twenties. Not only could he fly the heck out of these planes, he could land them as well under the most extreme circumstances, and do it safely. Motherfucker, he was good! Jeff was from Galveston and had been flying since his late teens. He had balls of steel and the capabilities to match. I had seen him fix a spewing gas line in the cockpit mid-flight. He was as mechanical as he was proficient behind the yoke. The boy was not afraid of anything. For that matter, none of us were, and that's probably what brought us all together. Jeff was special, however. I had witnessed him jump into a twin-engine plane he had never flown before, hot-wire it, fire it up, and point it toward the Mexican border in a moment's time. Like I said, the boy had balls of steel.

The first time I met Jeff was on a runway in Veracruz. Jeff had been hired by Jordan, another friend who, coincidentally, was also from Galveston. On this particular run, I had been stuck in Mexico with the load and waiting for two months or more. It was much too long. I was ready to get things moving and get the hell out of there. I had transported the weed out of the mountains of Oaxaca and trucked it to a stash house in Veracruz. This took months due to complicated logistics. Then I returned to the States to facilitate the transport of the load out of Mexico and into Texas. I could have sold insurance like my dad, but the revenue wasn't nearly as good, and there was no comparison to the excitement. There was nothing that captured my interest like smuggling.

Back in the States, I made constant calls to Boch in Mexico. It was his job to have the load ready and waiting on the airstrip. This segment of the journey was always a logistical nightmare as there were so many people to coordinate. One day he called me and said, "Dude, you need to get back down here. I cannot keep these motherfucking Mexicans in line." I immediately flew back down to Veracruz to resolve the bottleneck. The following days were endless, spent in multiple hotel rooms. The stress was building and building.

While in Veracruz, I took a nap one afternoon and woke up around six in the morning. I was surprised I was so exhausted that I slept through the night. I decided to go outside and greet the sunrise: seven o'clock came, then seven thirty, then eight. I was freaking out! No shit, I thought God had spoken and it was the end of the world. I rushed into the hotel room, quizzing anyone coherent, "What time does the sun come up?" In their weed-induced stupor, they all claimed, "By about seven or seven thirty." This was now becoming eerie; it was way past that. My anxiety was over the top. After pacing back and forth outside for a while, I went back in the room and told the guys to quit fucking with me. I was very agitated and said, "Come on, motherfuckers! When does the sun come up?" They said "Calm down, Dude. It will be here tomorrow morning about seven thirty." Guess I was just a little wound up.

This is how crazy and convoluted my existence had become. Everyone involved was smoking an extreme amount of weed and drinking tequila after tequila. This shit went on all day, every day. It was always difficult to keep this group of Mexican renegades focused on the project at hand. They continuously had way too much time on their hands, and getting fucked up was a huge priority. We were in the illegal drug business, and unfortunately, it went with the territory. Finally, I got those boys in line, but we still needed to wait for the plane to transport the weed back to the States.

Coincidentally, Mardi Gras was going on in Veracruz at that time. Boch, Ricardo and I decided to join in the festivities that were occurring throughout the city to give us something to do. As you might imagine, the town was alive with crowds of people in costumes. There was music, dancing in the streets, parades, colorful banners and flags, honking cars, and people strolling around in a drunken state. Nothing ever gets much crazier than Mardi Gras.

Eventually, Boch, Ricardo, and I got separated due to the large number of people at the event. I was meandering around the *zócalo,* beer in hand, just enjoying the festivities when I noticed the most beautiful woman sitting at a table with a group of men at one of the restaurants adjacent to the town square.

She appeared to be a wealthy woman who I assumed had probably come from Mexico City for the events. She was elegantly dressed and had a regal demeanor. This woman was incredibly good-looking with perfect makeup and hair and long painted nails. I was extremely attracted to her and circled the square multiple times, glancing over at her briefly, so I would not get caught staring as I passed her table.

Well, goddamn, if one of her gentleman friends didn't battle the crowd and introduce himself. I was blown away when he said, "My sister would like to meet you." No way, how could I be so fucking lucky? I told him, "Why of course," and proceeded to follow him back through the crowd to the awaiting *señorita*.

Oh, my god, she was even prettier close up. I stood in front of her and offered my hand as I introduced myself, hoping my feelings would not show through. She greeted me in Spanish and asked, "Won't you join us?" I was completely flattered and told her, "Of course, I would love to." I wanted to ensure that we spoke only in Spanish, so I told her I was German, assuming she wouldn't know that language. I was right; she couldn't speak German, so we conversed in Spanish the rest of the afternoon.

I was having a great time. There I was throwing back Cuba Libres with a beautiful woman at twilight in the *zócalo* in Veracruz; my Mardi Gras dreams had been fulfilled. This woman was perfect. The fact that she was maybe ten years older made her even more alluring. Again I had been right: she was visiting from Mexico City. We talked for at least two hours, and all the while I was convincing myself I would certainly be invited to her expensive condo for a late night romance. I was incredibly excited. Then unbelievably she took my hand and said, "Would you like to come to my hotel room?" Would I! I had to restrain my enthusiasm when I answered, "Well, of course. I would be honored."

We excused ourselves from the others and casually strolled hand-in-hand to her hotel. I could not have been prouder; I had the most beautiful woman on the square. As she led me up the stairs to her room, my sexual desire was mounting. When we passed through the door, she immediately guided me to the bed. I could not believe my luck. She pulled me to her, and we began to kiss passionately. When I reached up to caress her breasts, she gently pushed me away, and looking at me tenderly, said, "Sandy, there is something I need to tell you." I interrupted her quickly and said, "No, no, no, there is something I need to tell you first…I'm not German." As she continued looking at me, her eyes filled with tears and she said, "I'm not female." Confused, I asked, "What do you mean? What are these?" indicating her breasts with my hands, my mouth hanging open in disbelief. With tears then streaming down her cheeks she said, "We have our ways."

Motherfucker, I did not know what to do as I stumbled back, perplexed at this revelation. Oh, my god, I thought as I continued to move farther away. I wondered who the hell might have seen me come up to this room? Oh my god, what was I going to do? She cried harder and harder as I continued to move backward toward the door. "I got to go, I got to go!" I kept repeating. However, she was crying so hard that I started to feel sorry for her. I stopped myself at the door and felt the need to comfort her or him or them, so I paused a moment. "Let me just walk you downstairs to say goodbye," she kept begging me. There was no way I wanted to take any more chances that some of my friends might see me with this woman/man. I was mortified. However, she was crying so hard, I finally relinquished and said, "OK, walk me to the door." "Fuck, let me just get the fuck out of here," I thought to myself. Once to the front doors, I said "bye" and bolted into the street, looking around for anyone I knew. Fortunately, I didn't see any of my friends, so I just blended back into the crowd. Motherfucker, what a close call that was… but goddamn, he sure was pretty!

After our Mardi Gras adventure, we headed to our hotel to wait for the plane. Eventually, Jeff flew in, and the Mexicans and I loaded the twin engine with weed. It may not have been my most prudent move, but I was so ready to get the hell out of there, I decided to ride with the load, rather than wait for a commercial flight. I comfortably spread out over the top of the bales and hollered toward the cockpit, "When are the cocktails served?" In return, I got a roar of laughter. "Tray tables up and no smoking," the joking motherfuckers yelled back.

We crossed into the US safely, but unfortunately, our clandestine runway had been compromised. It was an extremely dark and clear night, and from above, you could see everything. The cops were easy to spot with their red-and-blue flashing lights. Then we had another problem: we were low on fuel. Jeff knew of a small airport ahead in Houston and concluded this was an option. Unfortunately, it soon became our only option, as we realized we were out of fuel. We decided to land, refuel, and then figure out our next move. We were full of weed, out of fuel, and in a bad situation.

The landing did the deciding for us. The right engine quit at touchdown. We had cut it much too close. We were safely on the ground, but unfortunately, the airport was closing, actually turning the lights off and shutting the pumps down as we pulled up to them, only one engine running. We were totally screwed! I made sure, from my position in the back of the plane, that the curtains were tightly closed to avoid bringing any additional attention to our predicament.

There was a second pilot named Frank on board. He got out and distracted the security guard on duty while Jeff and I taxied the plane to the darkest and most remote location we could find in the parking area. On board, we had the rudimentary two-way radios designed for cars that I mentioned earlier. There we were in downtown Houston with a thousand pounds of weed on board, stuck. Once the plane was parked, I grabbed a two-way radio and a car antenna, climbed up on the wing, and stood as straight and tall as I possibly could, pointing the antenna toward the stars. "Whiskey eleven, whiskey eleven, do you copy? Whiskey eleven, do you copy?" I shouted into the radio. (We always used some bogus call sign such as "whiskey eleven" to alert our ground crew.) The minutes ticked by and there was still no response. "Whiskey eleven, whiskey eleven, do you copy?" Shortly, a scratchy reply came back over the airwaves. "Whiskey eleven here; where are you guys?" I informed Jordan where we were and shouted, "Bring the fucking van!" Fifteen to twenty excruciating minutes passed, and Jordan finally arrived. He pulled up to the plane, and we immediately started unloading. We must have looked like honorary UPS delivery drivers, shuffling bale after bale from the plane to the van. In no time, we were gone, leaving the plane behind.

Jordan and I had been friends for a few years by then. I met Jordan in Mexico with another friend named Ralph. Ralph and Jordan had come to Mexico together to purchase weed and figure out how to get it across the border. One way or another, they ended up in Cholula and through some mutual friend found their way to my house. The three of us hit it off great, and another conspiracy was formed. I would supply the weed if they could truck it to the border. I would also complete the border crossing. My weed, my crossing, their trucking; it would be an uneven split monetarily. Despite this initial transaction, we all became great friends and equal partners in the smuggling business.

Jordan and Ralph both graduated from Southwest Texas State University in San Marcos. Once again, they were single, white, college-graduate Texas boys who were attracted to the money and adventure. We all fit the same profile exactly. Jordan was a sizeable guy with green eyes, curly brown hair, and a mustache. He had grown up in Galveston under the same circumstances I had in San Antonio. He was from a well-to-do family and neighborhood with all the associated manners and education. Ralph was small-framed with light eyes and blond, wavy hair. He was from Houston with a similar background. None of us ever really saw our involvement as criminal. It was the Cause we were vested in: sex, drugs, and rock 'n' roll.

I have to give credit to Jordan for introducing the first planes we used. There were many firsts. Ralph got his pilot's license first. Unfortunately for Ralph, he crash-landed the first plane Jordan had bought in a refueling attempt in Refugio, Texas. He was then the first to be arrested. This was the end of Ralph's smuggling career. A positive footnote, however; Ralph did not end up going to jail, though he endured a lengthy and extensive probation. As a result of his arrest, he decided to go back to school and earned his business degree, went to work for a large oil field supply company, made a few million dollars through salary and stock options, had a beautiful wife and child, and bought a million-dollar ranch in South Texas. All ended up pretty good for ol' Ralph.

On the other hand, Jordan and I maintained a "never say die" attitude. Well, we hadn't been caught…yet. Keep in mind: the laws were more lenient in 1980. Ralph had an airplane with a thousand pounds of weed on board and still only got probation. Ah, those were the good ol' days.

Sometime after Ralph's demise, Jordan and I eventually hooked up with Jeff. The planes we acquired got bigger and faster. Jordan and I both ended up getting our pilots' licenses together. We were quite a team. Jeff and Jordan would fly, and I would "catch" them on the ground; or Jeff and I would fly, and Jordan would do the "catching." It worked like a charm.

Jordan and I spent lots of crazy times together. One day, we decided to attend a police auction and ended up buying two matching police cars. The police decals were missing, although they both still had the spotlights attached at the doors and maybe an antenna or two. They were obviously unmarked fucking police cars as far as we were concerned. The two of us were absolutely enamored with our new purchases. We raced around, skidding to a stop, and spotlighting other cars as we sped by them. Oh, my god, we had us some fucking cop cars! Together, we were a dangerous duo.

One night, Jordan and I were celebrating his girlfriend's birthday. We were getting drunk on expensive champagne and pouring it down like water. Jordan suddenly suggested we drive our matching cop cars out into the country and do a little shooting with some of the guns he had collected in his arsenal. He was a real gun freak. Nothing to fear, Texas boys love guns; no criminal intent, but all animals needed to be on the lookout, especially varmints.

We loaded ourselves like mercenaries. I had two pistols in my belt and an HK 93 slung across my chest. I was undoubtedly and unmistakably "ready for bear," as we say in Texas. No telling what Jordan may have been packing. As I walked out the front door of his girlfriend's apartment heading toward my cop car, I heard, "Help! Help! I've been robbed!" Oh my god! "Could this have come at a better time?" I thought to myself. No fucking way! I ran over to the damsel in distress as she was still screaming, while simultaneously hollering back at Jordan, "Come on, Dude!" I approached the victim and asked her, "Yes, Ma'am, what seems to be the problem?" She may have responded, but I never heard a word she said. Was I dreaming? I was so excited, I couldn't contain myself. I was pacing back and forth, bouncing on the balls of my feet, rifle in hand. "Oh shit, baby, game fucking on," I convinced myself in my inebriated state.

I ran over and jumped into my cop car, fired it up, and slammed it into reverse. I squealed the tires as I gunned it backward, and then threw it into drive. I peeled out of the parking lot, in hot pursuit yet clueless about where I was headed or even what I was looking for. With spotlight glaring and tires squealing, I circled the block aimlessly. Jordan then appeared behind me in his matching cop car and pulled alongside, yelling through his passenger window, "Dude, what the fuck?" Glancing down at the arsenal around my belt, I replied, "Let's get the fuck out of here!" We turned off our spotlights after realizing the absurdity of our situation and sped away. I hated cops, but I sure enjoyed being one that night.

I kept that car for a couple of years as a backup and had fun driving it between Austin and Houston at a hundred-plus miles per hour, drunk and coked up, spotlighting multiple cars so they would pull over, allowing me to zoom by. One time, I even tried to pick up some whores on Sixth Street in this car, and the response was "Uh-uh, cowboy, I don't think so." I loved that cop car.

CHAPTER EIGHT

Well I stepped inside, and stood by the door
While a dark-eyed girl sang, and played the guitar
Hookers, and hustlers, filled up the room
I heard about this place they call the Spanish Moon

... *"Spanish Moon" by Lowell George*

As the flying picked up for Jordan, Jeff, and me, so did our capabilities, along with our reputations. Within our network of friends and associates, people started hiring us to bring their loads across the border. At this level, it became harder and harder to maintain the low profile mandated in such operations. After a while, the planes started getting bigger and the distances greater. We would travel to Belize and back and then to Jamaica and back to pick up loads for various characters. This is when what I would call the criminal aspect of my career started to unfold. It was 1981 and I was twenty-nine years old. We were beginning to meet people outside our white, middle-class Texas fraternity of friends.

In May of that year, I was hired to navigate a commercial Avianca jet carrying a load of weed out of Colombia and into the States. This obviously had to be a very secretive operation. We were still in the planning stage about where to land this big motherfucker. However, I was required to go to Bogotá and visit with the Avianca Airlines pilot ahead of time to work through the details. This was a goddamned commercial jumbo jet; well, hell yes, there would be some details to work out!

I made arrangements to meet with the pilot at the Bogotá Hilton. I booked a commercial flight and packed a bag. I decided to wear a jumpsuit with nametag and an American flag sewn to the sleeve, as it seemed like the perfect disguise. The only problem was it was the only thing I took. I thought I would be coming back on the Avianca jet the next day. The jumpsuit was royal blue with an Austin Boats and Motors patch displayed over one pocket. In one of our whacked-out moments, Jordan and I saw Clark wearing his jumpsuit and decided we both just "had to have one!" So we ordered two of them, patches and all. This was Clark's company and we wanted to give him a little recognition.

I arrived in Bogotá and checked into the Hilton, the swankiest hotel in town, wearing my jumpsuit. I was cool. I wouldn't be there long. After a few days, I was getting rather weary of my blue-collar attire. One would have thought I'd have bought a change of clothes. However, I was continually scheduled to leave "tomorrow." I did buy a pair of swim trunks at the hotel gift shop and wore them in the luxurious indoor pool while washing my underwear, socks, and tiresome jumpsuit. I did, eventually, meet with the Avianca pilot three or four days into my mission and discussed the particulars. After our meeting, he told me, "I'll get back to you soon." This, however, still left me in a holding pattern.

While waiting, I continually frequented the upstairs bar and other amenities the hotel offered. One evening, while throwing back my daily requirement of multiple cocktails, I met a gentleman who was visiting from the States. During our conversation, he discovered I spoke Spanish and informed me he had a Colombian "girl" coming to the hotel that evening. He asked if I would help translate for him. Since my schedule was fairly open, I told him I would be happy to oblige.

His hired Colombian girlfriend showed up, and I was surprised by the extent of her good looks and charming demeanor. She had an incredible smile. I also loved the way she dressed, as she was in fashionably conservative clothing, yet totally hot. I introduced myself as the translator and proceeded to do as requested. The exchange was extremely casual and curiously more like a "meet and greet" than a business transaction. Yet I was able to politely help them negotiate the fees and close the deal. Eventually, I pardoned myself and returned to my room.

After some time had elapsed, I became weary of sitting in my room and returned to the bar to buy a couple of drinks to go. With two drinks in hand, I headed back to the elevator. When the doors opened, there stood none other than the Colombian *señorita*! Laughter immediately erupted and conversation exploded between us. I handed her one of my drinks and asked if she would want to visit further in my room. She gracefully accepted.

I learned her name was Lidia. At some point during our brief romance, I asked her, "Why do you do what you do?" She looked at me directly and said without any hesitation, "Why do you do what you do?" This completely caught me off guard, and I wondered if it was that obvious I was a smuggler. I didn't quite know how to answer her question and wasn't sure if she was being defensive or was on to something. Regardless, we had a great time, and she ended up staying the night at no charge. My Colombian dreams had been fulfilled. Like Gabriel García Márquez, ah, "memories of my melancholy whores." Unfortunately, the business with the Avianca Airlines never came to fruition, and I departed Colombia within about a week. Not surprisingly, I never wore that fucking jumpsuit again.

A month after I returned from Colombia, a group from California approached me and asked us to help them with a similar deal. They had the plane but needed help getting their weed from Colombia back into the US. This new group was more flamboyant and mildly shady—outside our network style. They were coming into Texas from California, New York, and Colombia. This was the first time we saw people smoking crack, and they were doing it in their hotel rooms. We didn't recognize the danger because we didn't know what it was. However, they had big money, so we looked the other way.

There was also one more thing we didn't recognize soon enough: we were graduating into the upper echelon of smuggling. The DEA was also beginning to get wind of us, but greed was in charge. When a group of characters out of California was willing to pay us a quarter of a million dollars to help navigate them back into the US from Colombia, I, of course, couldn't help but volunteer for the project. It was all too appealing. Additionally, Jordan, Jeff, and I were always looking for more flight time, and this would be a run to Colombia, a new notch in my belt. There was no ranking or organization to our business; it was just the three of us. We were loosely organized and really just friends. The DEA apparently thought otherwise.

After a few test flights into the Austin, Houston, and a couple other airports, the Californians' plane, a Twin Turbo

Commander, was beginning to draw the attention of the DEA. Agents were placed at airports to scrutinize airplanes of this size and style. Simultaneously, we recognized the risk of this profile and decided to get the plane out of the country. Ultimately, we decided to take the big twin turboprop to Belize where it sat just long enough for Interpol to have been alerted. They tagged the plane "high alert status" throughout the rest of the world for suspicion of illegal activities. It took a bounty paid to the Honduran Government to get the plane released and flown to Costa Rica.

The first step for me was to fly to San Jose, Costa Rica, in preparation for the flight to Colombia. I caught a commercial flight from Houston to meet up with the other pilot and participants in this endeavor. After I arrived in San Jose, a customs official approached me in line and said, "*Señor* Stokes?" He gestured me out gracefully with his palm extended and proceeded to escort me through the customs process without any delays. We then went upstairs to a bar where my associates were having drinks with high-ranking customs officials. I was impressed—these Californians were well-connected. There was so much money in the drug trade at this time, it was not surprising to see government corruption firsthand. After salutations and drinks with the officials, we left for the hotel to scrutinize the maps and plot our course to Colombia. We had to figure out the refueling stops for the trip back into the US with a final destination outside of Houston. All was agreed upon, and we readied ourselves for our upcoming departure.

I returned to my hotel and found two maids cleaning my suite. There was a brief exchange between us, and they appeared to be somewhat intrigued with my Spanish. Surprisingly, after tidying my room, they both returned later and summoned me to the door. They asked if they could enter and ask me a question. I told them, "Of course, please come in," not knowing what on earth they might be requesting. They were giggling, yet very forthright in their communication. They asked me, "*Señor*, would you have sex with us?" I was dazzled as well as flattered. Well, hell yes, I would, "Now?" "No, no, no, *Señor*, we will return shortly after our shift." An hour or so later, there they were, ready to party. I was ready as well. How the hell does this shit happen to me? Nonetheless, I discovered I also loved Costa Ricans!

After spending a couple of days with "Doc" the pilot, I should have jumped on the first flight to Texas and never looked back. This motherfucker was a complete loose cannon and very unpredictable, not my kind of people. However, it wasn't my style to jump ship in the middle of a commitment. The morning of our departure arrived, and after taxiing down the runway of San Jose International, off we went to Colombia: Doc, Julio, and I.

Julio, who I had just met onboard, was the Colombian liaison. Doc was the lead pilot, and I was sitting right seat as the navigator. As the flight continued to unfold, the situation worsened. We started drifting off course little by little; however, when I reported this, Doc became aggressive, agitated, and basically unresponsive to my directives. Apparently, I was never in control of the navigation from the beginning. I smelled trouble at twenty thousand feet.

The weather then began to turn on us with rain and a few clouds, but nothing that aircraft couldn't handle. Yet Doc started freaking out. "I'm going to put this thing down, goddammit. I'm going to put this thing down," he began screaming. "No, no, no," I argued, "What the fuck are you thinking? We're fine! Just get back on fucking course, motherfucker!" But as stated, I was far from in control, and that was becoming more and more apparent as things continued to unravel. I should have been listening to that inner voice much earlier, but I didn't. I was focused on the money.

Apparently, we were somewhere over Panama, but at this point, it was just a peninsula from where I was sitting. Actually, I didn't know where we were, as he had been off course for so long. I just knew that we were not yet in Colombia, and Doc the Unpredictable was about to plant this big rig on some airstrip, in some country, somewhere. The good news was we landed safely. The bad news was it was a Panamanian Military Base. We were, subsequently, surrounded by a military platoon, immediately arrested, then confined. "Man, I should have listened to myself," I could hear echoing in my head.

We were loaded into the back of a large military vehicle with a few of the troops and driven to downtown Panama City where we were processed into the city jail and placed into what I would call a dungeon. It was as nasty as one can imagine: a cold, wet, dark, filthy cavern, not like the fine hotels to which I was accustomed. Some type of gruel was served in lieu of food and I even had to sleep on the floor. I had to wear the same shorts, shirt, and topsiders throughout my stay, and even developed some type of foot fungus that lasted for years.

The following week, I was interrogated repeatedly by the Panamanian police and shown photos of a large load of cocaine being taken off the plane. This was, of course, a complete fabrication because we had been heading *to* Colombia, not returning. They kept asking me in Spanish, "Where is the cocaine from? Who sold you the cocaine?" Apparently, they wanted to confiscate the nice big plane, thus, the photos of the coke. My Spanish was fluent and I simply replied, "What the hell are you talking about? I'm a surfer and was simply hitchhiking to a beach in Colombia." They were pretty upset when I said, "I think you guys put that shit on the plane."

Maybe I shouldn't have said that because then they were really furious. They shouted back at me, "Oh, so you think the Panamanian Government would stoop so low as to put cocaine on your plane?" I continued in Spanish, "Apparently, and by the way, I think I need an interpreter."

I was later moved from the dungeon to the standard cells upstairs where the rest of the population was held. This place looked like the hull of a ship, with cots hanging from the walls by chains. It was not pleasant by any means and not necessarily any cleaner, simply more social. However, everybody on our cellblock thought we were snitches. I never understood why, maybe it was the jet airplane. Whatever, we only made friends with a few and enemies with most others. It was a strange set of circumstances. Eventually, I got in a fistfight with one of the prisoners over a bed. I was aware from my previous time in Latin America that white guys were resented and considered *pinche gringos*. We were hated by most of the population, and I was as *gringo* as they came.

Though I was accustomed to resentment, my Spanish always became the equalizer. The population consisted of approximately 70% Panamanians, 20% Colombians, and 10% Americans. This was a unique blend of characters, stuck in similar circumstances, and we were only one floor of a six- or seven-story building. As far as I could tell, they had all of the Colombians and Americans on this particular floor. Yet we were a very eclectic group; some were standard low life criminals and others appeared to be regular guys. One of the Americans was the *maître d'* of the Waldorf Astoria in New York and another, a wealthy expatriate, who went by the name Bradley and owned a large sailboat anchored in Thailand. Bradley was a professional smuggler who was incarcerated for having presented Panamanian officials a bogus passport at entry. Brad was a funny fucker. We became good friends during our stay together.

Brad maintained a nonchalant attitude about our situation. He knew it was only a matter of time and money to get out of there. That was true; money bought anything and anyone in Panama, including the government. Eventually, both Brad and I did buy our way out, but not before we had a particularly funny experience.

I learned that on holidays in Central and South America, prisons allow the families of the inmates to participate in a celebration, usually held in the courtyard. The families of the local prisoners bring food and maybe a small gift for their loved one and partake of the day's events. I happened to be there on Father's Day, a particularly bad day for me, as I was unable to contact my dad, and he had no idea I was in a Panamanian prison. However, I thought it was a beautiful idea; it was all about family, very touching.

The prison officials had even put together a prison band for this event, so there was food, music and dancing. We didn't realize there was a special cell that adjoined the courtyard, kept separate from the rest of the prisoners. The day of the celebration, Brad and I discovered that this particular cell held all the transvestites and overt homosexuals. When the music started, the doors were unlocked and swung open. You would have thought they were debutantes coming down a spiral staircase greeting kings, but they were transvestites from *Celda* 13, giddy and ready to party! They came out in full drag, ready to dance, maybe even ready to perform other services. This was goddamned hilarious. They made their way to the dance floor in stockings and high heels, swishing their girly dresses. All were perfectly made up with coiffed hair. It was obvious they were having the time of their lives.

Brad, with a boyish and deviously cocked smile, looked at me and said, "Dude, when are you going to have another opportunity like this?" In grand style, Brad slid onto the dance floor and started to dance with the "girls." It was so goddamned funny; I was folded over with laughter. Brad was waving and mouthing at me, "Come on!" I couldn't help myself—he was right. When would you have another opportunity like this? It was so crazy! I straightened the dismal shirt I'd been wearing for the past thirty days, combed my fingers through my hair, and sashayed my cute little ass to the dance floor. I extended my hand and in Spanish asked one of the *putitos*, "May I have this dance?" Of course, I picked the prettiest one I could find. I danced like I'd never danced before, with beautiful *jotos* in full drag in the prison courtyard in downtown Panama City Prison on Father's Day. I could have danced all night!

Back in Houston, sometime later, I did meet up with Brad and helped him retrieve his sailboat out of Thailand—after we both had bought our way out of the Panamanian prison. All in a day's work. Ho-hum.

My release from the Panamanian prison came in early July 1981, about six weeks into my detainment. One day, I was summoned by the guards and escorted downstairs for a visitation. I was clueless about who it could be. It turned out to be a New York attorney named Shapiro. I had no idea who hired him, but he informed me I was soon to be released. This guy knew everything, including the fact that I had totally denied any involvement during the police interrogations. He even had copies of the interrogation transcripts the Panamanian police had compiled. He said, "Sandy, you're the only one who hasn't talked, and my clients are willing to pay $15,000 to get you out of here." I was very grateful, but still did not know whom to thank.

To my surprise, my dad showed up the next day. I had been missing more than a month by then. Everyone was worried. Jordan was particularly distraught because he knew I was going to Colombia and had never returned. He even resorted to holding séances in my closet in Austin, in hopes of reaching my spirit. Eventually, I got word to him of my whereabouts and predicament. He was just happy to hear I was alive and didn't know what else to do but inform my dad. Coincidentally, Jordan had retrieved $15,000 I had previously hidden in the back of my sock drawer and met my dad in San Antonio to further discuss this precarious situation. They were both only trying to help.

Again, I was summoned from my cellblock and escorted downstairs to the visiting room. There sat my dad. It was a tearful reunion. He was so perplexed to see me in those circumstances that it broke my heart. He immediately informed me, "Sandy, I have $15,000 in cash that Jordan gave me to help get you out." I said to him, "Sit tight, brother, an attorney showed up yesterday out of New York, and I am about to be released in the next few days." "Save my money," I told him. "We'll put it to better use." Even though my lifestyle and vocation were completely foreign to him, he was compassionate and accepting. I did ask him, "Will you please give me a couple hundred bucks, so I'll have a little jack until I get out of here?" I always talked to him in the vernacular. I don't know how the fuck he dealt with it.

As I have mentioned before, money bought you anything in a Panamanian prison. I could have probably bought two whores and a private room had I so requested. What I did with my two hundred dollars, though, was to request take-out Chinese food for thirty. It cost me all two hundred dollars, but it was worth it. It allowed me to invite all the Colombians and Americans on my cellblock. Crazy! Once the food arrived, the guards escorted my selected bunch of criminals down to the cafeteria for a dinner to remember.

Before I boarded my plane out of Panama, I was asked by the attorney to stop by a hotel room in Panama City and visit a gentleman by the name of Vicente. It couldn't have been any more clandestine, and I didn't know what to think. However, I was only happy to oblige my new favorite attorney. Incredibly, Vicente seemed to be in Panama solely on my behalf. I was given the hotel name and room number by the attorney and traveled to the hotel by cab. I found the room and knocked on the door. It opened slowly and there stood an extremely large, fat, hairy, barrel-chested Italian with a rotund belly, and multiple gold-chains hanging around his neck. He stuck his hand out to shake mine and invited me in. Goddamn, I was nervous! In a strong, guttural Italian accent he murmured, "Come on in, Sandy. It's a pleasure to meet you," straight out of a Godfather movie.

I was admittedly scared. This guy was a total New York, Italian-style mobster. I had no idea this trip happened to be a mob-related exercise—no clue; but hey, to my surprise, after we sat and talked for a while, I felt surprisingly comfortable. My code of silence, it seemed, coincided with that of the mafia. I learned it all from black-and-white movies; you never talk. Apparently, I was a player. Vicente thanked me for not ratting on anyone, wished me the very best of luck, and escorted me to the door to say goodbye. I left the hotel room a little shaken but intact. I was back on the streets and now leaving the country because of his cash and rescue. He seemed like a pretty good guy…I guess. I never worked with this group again, but that was not the last time I heard about them.

Cautiously exuberant, my father and I boarded a commercial jet back to Houston the next day. I never heard from Julio or Doc again. However, the DEA was kind enough to visit with me in the not-too-distant future and inform me of the demise of Julio after he returned to his home in Colombia; but nothing about Doc, thank goodness. I presume Doc had been working with the DEA prior to the events of Panama due to his behavior on the flight to Colombia. I suspect he never intended to go to Colombia and had some sort of international immunity, no matter where he put that plane down. I was never to know what had actually transpired with that crazy fuck.

There is one anecdotal story about the confiscation of the plane. Less than a year after I had returned from Panama, I read in the newspaper that General Noriega had formed a coup that had overthrown the government of Panama and ousted the previous president by the name of General Omar Torrijos. General Torrijos was fleeing to Colombia, and while in route, was blown up in mid-air in a Twin Turbo Commander, just like the one they confiscated from us. Crazy.

General Noriega was, subsequently, arrested during the US invasion of Panama. The invasion was prompted after a US Senate panel was convened to investigate his involvement in the international drug trade. The lead testimony before the Senate judicial panel was presented by a fellow Texas smuggler I knew named Steven Kalish. After the invasion of Panama, General Noriega was arrested and brought to Miami where he faced drug charges. He was put on trial and convicted, and is still incarcerated today. Noriega brought down by a Texas smuggler in his late twenties—still hard to believe.

I still speak with Steven's partner, Olan, from time to time. He was also from Texas, but had been "on the run" for almost twenty years in Colombia before finally deciding it was time to turn himself in. After Olan negotiated his surrender, the FBI flew down to Panama in a private jet to pick him up. Olan complained to me later that the jet they used was a third of the value or luxury of the previous jets he had owned. He was a little disappointed.

With my Panamanian incarceration, my low profile cover had been totally blown. I had finally made it onto the radar of the DEA. Had I given up my smuggling career after Panama, I probably would have made it through the gauntlet unscathed; but my assessment, at the time, indicated that this was simply another little bump in the road. Motherfucker, was I wrong.

Jordan and I had both heard through various sources that the DEA was watching us. What that meant to us was we just had to be more careful. It was the cat-and mouse-game, and we loved playing it. Jeff had DEA following him in and around Galveston. Jordan had ended up with the head of the Austin DEA in his car trying to negotiate some weed deal; fortunately, he grew suspicious and ended it. Then I had the Panamanian incident. The noose was slowly tightening around us. Regardless, the planeloads of weed continued.

CHAPTER NINE

It's so easy to slip
It's so easy to fall
And let your memory drift
And do nothin' at all
All the love that you missed
All the people that you can't recall
Do they really exist at all

Well my whole world seems so cold today
All the magic's gone away
And our time together melts away
Like the sad melody I play

… *"Easy to Slip" by Lowell George*

The business as we knew it had changed, and the DEA was beginning to get a foothold. We had spread ourselves far too thin and had become involved in too many circles of smugglers and dealers. Our names kept popping up repeatedly as one by one people were getting busted. Everyone was now cutting deals with the cops and ratting on all of their closest friends. Cooperation was becoming second nature because the authorities were mandating such long prison sentences.

Cocaine had now begun to rear its ugly head, and just about everyone I knew under forty was completely out of his or her fucking mind. I didn't know anyone who wasn't carrying a few grams around in his pocket and wouldn't offer me a bump or two. It was ridiculous: after lunch, after dinner, or just driving around. Coke was everywhere. It was the end of the fun and peace-loving drug era as we knew it.

Cocaine had permeated the entire culture and turned everything on its head. Crack or freebase, as it was originally called, was almost commonplace, and now it had infected our bunch, including myself. Though I abused cocaine, my business remained focused on weed even though more kilos of cocaine could fit on a plane than weed, and more money could be made as a result. In addition, everyone was addicted to it, so the demand was high. However, the transport of cocaine was far too dangerous and I was still primarily invested in the Cause. Unfortunately, the Columbian and Mexican smugglers had very little respect for life and had turned the whole business criminal. They had taken over the major supply lines from the white Texas boys that I represented.

By this time, late 1981, the culture was sex, drugs, and rock 'n' roll squared. We were using every means of transportation available to smuggle. We had airplanes, sailboats, shrimp boats, sea-going barges, and semi trucks and trailers, all stuffed to the brim with weed. In both stash houses and my own garage, there were tens of thousands of pounds of weed stacked to the ceiling in bales and as much as a half-million dollars in my clothes dryer, for lack of any better place to put it. I had U-Haul wardrobe boxes full of cash—a fascinating spectacle. We were out of control on cocaine, pills, girls, and weed. As you might imagine, it wasn't long before we all started to slip up.

Jeff belly-landed and burned a Twin Commander plane in a field in Florida, after a landing gear malfunction as he flew back from Jamaica. Jordan got caught up in the same smuggling conspiracy. Both he and Jeff found themselves together in a federal courtroom in Houston. Similar circumstances had Clark and me sitting together at the defendant's table in another federal courtroom in Austin, represented by two partnered lawyers from the same firm. Clark and I had been arrested together on a trumped-up cocaine charge about the same time as Jeff's and Jordan's conspiracy charge.

Clark had been helping me maintain my fleet of vehicles and numerous boats for years; however, he ultimately paid a substantially high price for his minimal involvement in what the DEA christened "The Harry Russell Stokes Criminal Organization." We likened it to more of a "disorganization" than anything organizational. Being the cynical fuck that he was, Clark always chastised me for never receiving his copy of the "Disorganization Newsletter."

Prior to our arrest, Clark and I had been hanging out at his boat dealership when an ex-employee showed up and wanted to buy a couple kilos of cocaine. Neither Clark nor I really sold coke, but if somebody needed some, we always welcomed the chance to make a little additional cash. As I have mentioned, coke was everywhere, and two kilos were readily available. I knew plenty of people who had it, so I got him some. A few months went by before the guy called back and said he only wanted an "eight ball", which I delivered to him and some of his friends at Applebee's. Clark also gave him a little on another occasion.

Several months later, I was asleep at my house in South Austin. It was early, just as the sun was coming up. I was sleeping soundly when an explosion suddenly rocked the house. It turned out that DEA agents had kicked in both front and back doors, shattering glass and crashing the wood panels to the floor. They charged in from all sides of the house, and before I knew it, I had ten of these motherfuckers dressed in attack gear with guns drawn standing around my bed. They had all sorts of guns, big and bigger. I looked around at them while trying to come to and said, "Uh, may I help you?" With guns pointed at my head, they shouted at me, "Are you Harry Russell Stokes?" "Depends on who's asking," I replied while facing the multiple gun barrels. "We've got a warrant for your arrest, so get the fuck out of bed!" I tried to maintain my composure and asked, "Would somebody please pass me my robe?" They moved their guns in closer and yelled, "Just get the fuck out of bed. You're under arrest for possession of cocaine and an intent to distribute." Uh-oh, they had me. I suddenly recognized one of the fat fuck agents from the transaction at Applebee's. Apparently, Clark's ex-employee had been an informant.

As I stood there naked, one of them threw me a pair of jeans that were wadded up on the floor and said, "Just put these on!" I pulled on my jeans in front of them and slipped into a t-shirt I found on the floor. They immediately grabbed me and cuffed my hands behind my back. Next, they proceeded to tear my house completely apart. They pulled the doors off their hinges, hammered into the walls, uprighted my bed, and emptied all my drawers onto the floor. However, they were not successful in finding any more drugs. They had missed them, I am pleased to report. I had nothing of consequence, but they missed them just the same. My stash was in the ceiling light above my bed, dumbasses.

Regardless of how stupid I thought they were, I was about to have a pretty miserable morning, not to mention the next few years. "Game on motherfuckers," I confidently said to myself as I was escorted out the door in handcuffs and placed in the rear of a now familiar Crown Vic. It kind of reminded me of my own cop car, however unfamiliar I was with the backseat. I learned later that Clark had awakened simultaneously to the same circumstances.

After my arrest, I found myself on the stand in an Austin courthouse for an arraignment hearing. My father and grandmother were present to help me get released from jail. The DA and the DEA were relentless in their attempts to keep me locked up. The DEA was regurgitating data to the judge about my continued smuggling activities while I had been released on a previous bond for the same charge. This was true; however, there was no concrete evidence. When the judge was announcing the amount of my new bond, the DEA and DA contested. Therefore, the judge continued to raise it from $50,000, to $75,000, then to $100,000. Each time the judge raised the amount, my grandmother raised her finger, as if at an auction, claiming she would take the new bid. It was a beautiful sight to behold from where I was sitting. The cops were furious! That, my friends, is one bad motherfucking grandmother.

While fresh out on my new bond, I decided I needed to take a trip to Port Aransas, a small resort town on the Texas Gulf coast. I was driving my diesel Cutlass with installed radiotelephone. These were the first car phones and very few had them. I was all liquored up and coked up and decided to shoot my new pistol out the window of my moving vehicle. I had never shot it and wanted to see how it felt. I was out in the middle of fucking nowhere, and didn't know that all the land around me was a federal game preserve. Whoops! I hit the button for my power window and extended my pistol, "Bam, bam, bam, bam, bam," I let loose into the night. Before I knew it, flashing police lights were on my ass. Apparently, there had been a game warden hiding under a small bridge, looking for poachers. Well shit, seemed like I fit the profile.

He pulled me over and I was once again freaking out. Out on bond, drunk, coked up, and firing a pistol out my window... what the fuck was I thinking? Boch was with me and did not have a current visa for the US. Both of us just knew we were fucked. I was subsequently arrested and taken to the local police station in Refugio, Texas. I told the judge on duty that night that I wasn't poaching, just trying out my newly acquired pistol because I had thought it was a great safe place to do so, out the window of my speeding vehicle. I was in South Texas; cowboys, handguns, and hard liquor were commonplace. "No big deal your honor. I'm sorry." I was assessed a $145 fine, they handed my gun back to me, and the next thing we knew, we were back in the Cutlass hauling ass toward the beach. Boch, to say the least, was a bit miffed at me. Fortunately, the cops never asked for his ID, they didn't search the car, and there was no computer database to reveal I was freshly out of jail and on bond. Crazy! It was party time in Port A.

As mentioned, Austin was under siege from cocaine and drug abuse. Of course, I was a big part of the blame. To illustrate how bad it had become, our lawyers were bountifully snorting cocaine throughout our entire trial. It was not uncommon for both attorneys to take multiple snorts with us during recess for lunch and then return to the courtroom for oral arguments in the afternoon. I even paid them in cocaine. As a side note, my attorney, Mark Conan the Barbarian, quit the business at the end of my trial and entered into rehab. To say the least, none of the four of us—Jordan, Jeff, Clark, or me—fared too well at the outcome of our separate trials. Federal Prison, Big Spring, Texas, "Here we come!"

I was first to blaze the trail to Big Spring. I made it before the rest of my astute colleagues because my trial was the first to conclude. However, I was not one of the fortunate ones who got to drive up in a limo. I was considered a flight risk by the judge and taken away in handcuffs by two US Marshalls, straight from the courtroom at the moment of sentencing. This all happened real fast. I immediately found myself in the back seat of another Crown Victoria driven by the same US Marshalls, who now escorted me on a thirty-minute drive to a real live maximum-security prison outside of Austin called Bastrop Federal Prison.

I was promptly marched in, stripped of everything, body searched—internally and externally—then dressed in an ill-fitting set of khakis. It was a humbling experience. After being fingerprinted, photographed, re-clothed, and re-searched, I was given bed sheets and a blanket and escorted to my new living quarters. My day wasn't going so well, and I wasn't quite sure what next steps the Man had in store for me. I had always been quite the control freak, and now all of my controlling power was completely stripped away.

Prisons such as these were scored on a security scale from one to ten, and I believe this place had recently been rated an eleven. It was the home of the Texas Chain Saw Massacre murderer, if that gives any insight about the severity of this lockdown, located in the eastern hills outside of beautiful downtown Austin. Was this some kind of joke?

After a few days of trying to get acclimated, I was put through numerous assessments with various prison administrators, doctors, case managers, and psychologists—all employees of the Bureau of Prisons. It soon became obvious to the administrators that I didn't belong to any particular group of prisoners currently residing there: no gang affiliation, no tattoos, no nothin'. Due to my social status and educational background, the majority of prison officials felt that I might be better suited drinking hot tea on a verandah somewhere with my little pinky sticking out. I had to agree. I'll never forget the moment when the prison psychologist asked me, "Have you run into anybody else from Terrell Hills since arriving?" He didn't think so. I was a stranger in a strange land.

After six long weeks in this hellhole, I was on my way to Big Spring. I was more than happy to hear that news! I didn't really know much about Big Spring, other than I was about to exchange a maximum-security prison for a minimum-security prison. What I didn't know was that I was about to be enrolled in prison "diesel therapy" for the transfer. "Diesel therapy" translates to an excruciatingly long, labouring bus tour of the federal prison system. Oh, my fucking god! I was handcuffed, shackled, marched, and loaded onto a prison bus for a long and slow ride from Austin to Texarkana.

Once on the bus, I was handcuffed and shackled to the guy next to me. It was fucked up! They distributed baloney sandwiches in paper bags and told us, "Enjoy!" These had to be eaten while bending over our laps because our handcuffed wrists were fastened to a chain wrapped around our waists and secured to our feet. One word comes to mind: motherfucker! Upon arrival at the next prison, it was all of the previous induction processes repeated: fingerprinted, photographed, strip-searched, and then re-dressed. Oh yeah, I was really loving this. A few weeks of stay in that prison, I was again cuffed, shackled, marched, and loaded back onto the bus. Give me a fucking break! Off I went to another prison.

Next stop was El Reno, Oklahoma. Again, it was a long, slow, lumbering bus ride with the same stale baloney sandwiches. Guards were positioned with shotguns in the front and rear of the bus, and wire mesh covered each window. I was a fucking convict! There were some murdering motherfuckers on board as well. They were handcuffed with little black boxes between their wrists to secure them even more than the rest of us. However, these were now my new friends. The guy chained to my right introduced himself as Eric and announced it was his 21st birthday. How sad was that? We all chatted, joked, and even traded spoiled fruit for the dreaded baloney sandwiches to distract us from our current misery as we sputtered down the highway. What strange circumstances. I stared out the window at the passing terrain for hours upon hours, handcuffed, shackled, and dressed in a goddamned orange jumpsuit, idly pondering my present situation—fucking horrific!

At some point along the way, I was even bused back to San Antonio and loaded onto a prison jet at the international airport. Can you imagine? My hometown! I was cuffed, shackled, and still wearing my orange jumpsuit, chained to thirty other prisoners and escorted at gunpoint through the terminal. I was afraid one of my parents' friends or someone else might recognize me. What a fucking nightmare!

Upon arriving at El Reno, Oklahoma, I went through all the same processing. How many photos and fingerprints do they fucking need? Why didn't they just bring yesterday's? This motherfucking endurance trip took four goddamned months. I saw the inside of so many nasty ass prisons; it was unbelievable. It was definitely not the kind of trip you would ever want to book twice. (Unfortunately, I did.)

El Reno, without a doubt, resembled the worst prison movie I had ever seen—only now I was starring in it. Inside, there were multiple-tiered cells, just like Alcatraz. There was continuous shouting and crying from the inmates, echoing off the hard brick walls. There were also hands protruding between the bars with mirrors to communicate with the adjacent cells, and strings thrown over the various levels to retrieve cigarettes, notes, and even drugs. It was definitely the big house. I might as well have been in a zoo with gorillas.

After a couple of months of this crazy bus tour, I came to the conclusion that if I didn't change my perspective, I would only grow more cynical. Therefore, I took the approach of an outside observer. As a result, the surrounding environment became academic. My new approach was to watch this ride and simply roll with it. I knew I would not be there forever, so let's "roll, baby, roll." I needed to adapt, and that's just what I did. Bring it on, motherfuckers!

I began to envision myself as a reporter. There were all sorts of different people I never intended to get to know, but what the fuck, why not try and broaden my horizons? I even met Billy Sol Estes, a larger-than-life con man from West Texas, who gained notoriety back in the sixties through his alleged relationship with Lyndon B. Johnson. He was even supposedly affiliated with the assassination of President Kennedy. When would you ever get the opportunity to visit face-to-face with a guy like that outside of prison? Actually, I mingled with a lot of famous criminals along the way, including Jim Baker. Billy Sol was only one of many.

I never saw myself as a criminal, but more as a political prisoner. It was all about the Cause. There were, undoubtedly, plenty of other regular guys imprisoned alongside me in the same unfortunate circumstances. However, rather than commiserate about this bullshit, I decided instead I would embrace this unique situation. It was still prison, and certainly it could get ugly, but only if I let it. I was never in a fight and never became someone's bitch. Admittedly, I was one lucky motherfucker to have visited the dark side and returned unscathed, with my sense of humor still intact.

After the hell of El Reno, I was once again chained, shackled, and loaded back onto the prison bus for the trip to Big Spring, Texas. After the same moaning, arduous trip, the prison bus doors finally swung open, and I had arrived. Even with my lengthy travel agenda, I was there before Clark, Jordan, and Jeff. I was, once again, fingerprinted, photographed, and strip-searched, and then welcomed to Big Spring. I had previously arranged for all of my clothes and toiletries to be sent ahead from Austin via mail, and they were waiting for me upon my arrival. I even had my tennis racquet! After gathering all my belongings, I was escorted to my "suite" at the Sunrise Unit.

They had to be kidding; it was a fucking hotel room! To my surprise, there were two double beds, a desk, a couple of chairs, a chest of drawers, and a goddamned lamp, plus an adjoining Hollywood bath. The bath included a private shower and dual sinks, all beautifully tiled and in immaculate order. I was totally blown away. After unpacking my bags, I stretched out across my new bed, and reached over to the end table, intending to make a call for room service when I discovered: no goddamned telephone. Oh well, I let my resentment pass, and after a long exhale, closed my eyes and dreamed of naked girls until the next morning sun. Crazy.

Morning came and I arose. I was hungry, so I walked over for some breakfast. I found the mess hall and went through the line as if I were at Luby's Cafeteria. Astonishingly, the coffee and food were quite palatable. I sat casually at a four-top and surveyed my new surroundings. Things were quite a bit different from the previous locations I had visited. Where the fuck were the rifle-toting, uniformed guards and dangling keys? Where were the *chulos* and their white supremacist counterparts? Didn't anybody have a tattoo here? Where the fuck were they? "Am I really still in prison?" I pondered, as I sat there sipping my coffee, maybe with my pinky extended, dressed in my blue jeans and Patagonia sports shirt.

After breakfast, I returned to my room, brushed my teeth, and gathered myself. With nothing else looming on my agenda, I felt it might be time for a little tennis. I was ready for a walk—why the heck not? After a comfortable four-block stroll, I spotted them: three perfectly maintained tennis courts with surrounding bleachers. Was I losing my mind? There they were though, filled with plenty of players knocking the ball around. There was not a fence or a prison guard in sight. As I approached the courts, I thought I was beginning to smell a very familiar odor. Was I dreaming? There were spectators on the bleachers: laughing, joking, reading magazines, sunning…and smoking weed? No fucking way! Were there drinks to be served later? Well, indeed there were. I could not believe this shit. It was totally absurd.

Big Spring, Texas, was home of a federal detention facility located on a converted World War II air force base, far out in West Texas. They called it a prison camp, more commonly referred to as a country club prison. There were no fences or walls, no locked doors, no guard towers, and few if any prison guards. There was nothing that even resembled a prison. It was set up on the honor system and you had to agree not to run off. You could, of course, but you had to promise you wouldn't.

This is the place where the courts sent white-collar, nonviolent types of criminals, and there were plenty of those: bankers, savings and loan executives, stockbrokers, swindlers, doctors, politicians, prime ministers, and county commissioners. There were plenty of smugglers and drug lords as well. Just about any nonviolent offender who had found himself on the wrong side of the law ended up at Big Spring.

From my assessment, it appeared that the courts got it right about 99 percent of the time. However, 98 percent of those all maintained their innocence. There were people from all walks of life and from every country and ethnicity imaginable. Some convicts flew in on their own private jets while others rolled up with strippers and had to be poured from their limos, empty whiskey bottles clanging on the pavement, as they stumbled out. Big Spring was a far cry from anywhere USA, and it always involved a long, arduous, and anxious trip with plenty of time to get drunk or fucked up.

The physical layout of Big Spring was on at least twenty acres of land. The cafeteria or mess hall was located at the southern end of the prison, whereas the auditorium and gymnasium sat at the northern end. The tennis courts and running track were situated at the perimeter of the campus along with the baseball field. It was an air force base with lots of room to move around. Everywhere you went required a fairly healthy walk, much like a college campus.

The living quarters at Big Spring were two elongated, three-story masonry buildings facing each other with a large parking lot dividing them. Nobody had a car, so the parking lot remained empty except for maybe one of the service or landscape vehicles operated by the detainees. The grounds were meticulously maintained by the inmates themselves. The dormitory with its back facing the west was called Sunset, and the one with its back facing the east was called Sunrise. Each building had about fifty private rooms per floor with every two rooms sharing a Hollywood-style bath. There were also four additional exterior rooms with private bath on each floor that included an outside balcony. These rooms were just as the cadets and officers of the prior air force base had left them—immaculately clean.

There was also a prison commissary where you could buy everything from cookies, crackers, and candy to canned goods, fresh avocados, tobacco, razors, and even tennis balls. How bizarre, it was a fucking convenience store! There were schools and a legal library, even a flight simulator where I could practice instrument approaches and long overseas trips, if I pleased. You could even take the written exam to acquire a private pilot's certificate. Could this be real? Many classes were available, including Spanish, religion, and computer science, with college credits attainable for most of them. In addition, there were pay phone banks to stay in contact with your loved ones or your attorney, if needed.

The amenities at Big Spring included a gymnasium with weight room, a full basketball court, a volleyball court with regulation nets and balls, a putting green with golf clubs and golf balls, a couple of baseball diamonds with surrounding dugouts and bleachers, baseball supplies to create as many as four teams, tennis courts, a swimming pool, horse shoe pits, a running track, a vegetable garden, and European bocce ball courts for the Euro detainees. There was also a clubhouse with pool tables and Ping-Pong and a big-screen TV with cable. Had I arrived at the Golden Door Spa?

The number of activities I chose to participate in was almost comedic. I had abs classes with a trainer, a running coach, and even a professional tennis coach from Dallas. I played a lot of tennis, as much as six hours a day. You can only imagine the great tan I acquired.

Big Spring not only looked like a college campus, but it had the feel of one as well. It was so incredibly casual that some of the guys had their girlfriends sneak in for an overnight stay. You could hear the girls giggling and scampering down the halls in the middle of the night. Some of the inmates also snuck off the compound at night and ran into town to buy bottles of liquor to re-sell to their buddies. It was an adult summer camp full of juvenile delinquents.

In addition, no one wore prison uniforms; rather, everyone was dressed in regular street clothes, all brought from home. Most inmates wore blue jeans or shorts and pullovers or button downs. You could be as casual as you wanted in tennis shorts and sandals or even swim wear. The only exceptions were the guards and administrators, who wore the Bureau of Prisons uniform. Somebody had to look like they were in charge.

Actually, the entire prison camp was run mostly by prisoners, with minimal overview and minimum prison staff. Some of the staff members were tolerable and others were not. Most all of them, however, were on a first-name basis with the prisoners. The staff was mainly made up of ex-military, who had served in Vietnam and after release were simply looking for jobs. Some were women, and there was a huge shortage of those. Regardless of their actual appearance, they all were a welcomed presence. On more than one occasion, the women guards got caught up in sexual relations with the inmates. I chose not to get involved, but one of my friends actually ended up marrying a prison guard.

Work was required from all of the inmates at Big Spring and there was a litany of things to choose from, depending on what you wanted to do. There was landscaping, painting, carpentry, electrical repair, housekeeping, administration, dishwashing, cooking, and even factory work, if you needed to earn some money. The factory made harnesses and even fatigues for the contras of Nicaragua. I can't even begin to explain that one. The salary was nine cents an hour, which sounded like indentured servitude to me. Thank God, I still had a wad of cash stashed at the house.

I landed a job in the kitchen preparing salad for four hundred inmates. The cafeteria was large enough to serve approximately two hundred people at a sitting. This was not a typical prison mess hall, since it had previously been a full-blown operational US air force base. There were only five paid staff in the cafeteria, and the rest of the workers were inmates. I was the salad chef. It was as if I worked in a restaurant, a big one, so my responsibility was substantial.

Every morning, I would wake up early and head to the mess hall. I had coffee and toast and a few laughs with the prison officials and the rest of my crew. We would then meander back to the salad-making section, which had large stainless steel tables and adjoining sinks and rinse basins. We washed spinach, cut celery, peeled carrots, etc., to serve our large group. With my team of three or four, it was never too daunting a task, and we could be done by eight. Then it was off to the tennis courts for another full day of fun in the sun.

The menu was similar to that of any cafeteria food with one twist: it gave you incredible gas. Shortly after the arrival of one of my partners, Lanny, he confided in me, "This food tends to give me gas. Does it you?" I thought I was going to burst with laughter. "No kidding!" was my response. It affected everybody the same. It was incredible the amount of gas this food produced. It was kind of scary and became rather worrisome. We all wondered if it would stop after release from Big Spring? Even though I worked inside the cafeteria, it was a struggle trying to figure it out. Was it a conspiracy? Were they secretly dousing the food with some additive before it reached us? We never knew, and the farting continued at ridiculously high levels. It was a fart fest.

After a few weeks at Big Spring had gone by, Clark arrived. Oh, my god, I couldn't believe it! I greeted him in the vernacular, "Clark, you motherfucking son of a bitch, get the fuck over here and give yo' motherfucking brother a hug! Goddammit man, I can't believe you're here!" I was dancing around and shouting out multiple vulgarities. "Fuck, I can't believe it," I repeated over and over again! He was completely freaked out and totally speechless. Clark seemed numbed by his new surroundings, and I was not making him feel much better. I was way too happy for his liking. He didn't know I was about to grab him by the arm and escort him outside to the balcony to stick a joint in his mouth. "Smoke on this, motherfucker!" This was more than he could take, "Are you serious?" he asked with a deer-in-the-headlights expression plastered all over his face. "Yeah man, relax, it's totally cool!" I'm sure he was thinking back to the last time I used that same line, and look where he now found himself. Here we were, though, together again. I smelled a guacamole party at hand.

I can honestly say, here was an innocent man, a stand-up motherfucker, inadvertently pulled into the legal system. He was in prison on my behalf, caught in the web of the federal courts, the War on Drugs, and the bullshit that went with it. I couldn't have felt worse. We both had been put through the wringer; only I was a bit guiltier, especially in relation to Clark.

Clark did one hell of a heroic move while under cross-examination from the federal prosecutor. Throughout the proceedings, the prosecutor continued to harass Clark about his involvement in the "Harry Russell Stokes Criminal Organization," demanding to know if he was part of it. Additionally, the prosecutor was trying to get Clark to say that he had gotten the cocaine from me. Clark raised his head slowly, stared the prosecutor straight in the face, and simply said, "I refuse to put a good friend of mine in the same predicament I find myself right now." I imagine the prosecutor was mighty stunned that someone would put their loyalty before their own self-interest. How often does that happen? What an incredibly brave thing for Clark to say given the certainty of the outcome—prison time.

I cannot overemphasize how frightening and anxiety-provoking it was to check into federal prison. I was even a little anxious myself. Clark's demeanor was very typical. You didn't know what to expect, and there was always the lingering thought that your release might be a lifetime away. However, the irony for us was that, after we settled in a bit, we were sort of back in our old life: all our old buds were there, everyone was still smoking weed, there was alcohol available, as well as food, snacks, and soft drinks, much like the life we had just left. The difference was now we were trapped in a sports facility and couldn't go home. It was strange, and even stranger how easy it was to acclimate after the initial shock wore off. Clark acclimated quickly and his humor caught up as well.

I got Clark a job working with me in the salad department, and that in itself was comical. I mean, there I was in prison working together with one of my best buds; it was damn funny. One morning, there was a standard meeting of the cafeteria employees and staff, and all were in attendance. A guard by the name of LaCerno was conducting the meeting and covering various topics about upcoming events. He asked for volunteers to help put up Christmas decorations. I was paying little attention to the content of the meeting, as I had already finished with the salad prep and was dressed in my tennis shorts and shoes, ready to make a beeline to the courts. I was chatting with another buddy when Clark tapped me on the shoulder and said to me, "Sandy, LaCerno just called your name." I immediately raised my hand and shouted "here!" Little did I know, I had just volunteered for the Christmas decorations and tree assembly.

LaCerno paused and said incredulously, "Stooooakes?" in his heavy Hispanic accent, likely imaging the self-proclaimed kingpin hanging tinsel on the tree. Clark thought this was the funniest prank of his entire stay.

Shortly after Clark's arrival, Jordan and Jeff checked themselves in as well. There we were, the four of us together again, incredibly sitting around the pool on beach blankets. Crazy. The fact that we would even have beach blankets, swim trunks, and sandals was even more absurd, but there we were at the pool, smoking cigarettes, sipping cocktails, and chatting about current events. An old Bob Dylan song came to mind, as I looked around, still sprawled out on my beach towel: "You know, I just can't help it if I'm lucky."

Big Spring also had an auditorium where various well-known bands played. Stevie Ray Vaughn came off tour and stopped by the prison for a benefit concert, after one of his buds had called him from the prison camp and asked if he would pay us a visit. That was a great concert. I also called a good friend of mine Don Bennett, with the Marcia Ball Band. Don and I had kept in close contact through the mail and with a phone call now and then. I asked him, at one point, if he and the rest of his band would agree to the same benefit concert scenario. He told me, "Sandy, I'll put it on the schedule." A month or so passed, and during one of their tours, The Marcia Ball Band showed up one Saturday night and played a three-hour benefit concert. They brought the house down.

I have an 8x10 photograph on my office wall that was taken backstage in the auditorium that night. In it are Don Bennett and I, plus a couple of other incarcerated friends. We were all dressed in jeans and polo shirts with white Styrofoam cups in our hands and smiles on our faces. We could've been backstage anywhere.

There were many concerts performed for us during our stay. If I listed all of the acts, it would sound like a Grammy Awards ceremony. The rock 'n' roll business and the drug business were linked in blood, and our brothers were never shy in their support of us. There was no shame in our predicament. At my request, Don smuggled in a Timex Iron Man watch, a new pair of running shoes, and maybe even some weed. This was strictly forbidden, as all incoming items had to be processed through appropriate prison channels. I guess it was still my nature to circumvent all authority at every opportunity.

One morning, a few of us were sitting around having coffee before work and making conversation. It was a varied group of inmates. I was talking about my trip to the Panamanian prison when suddenly one of the guys across the table stood up in surprise and asked, "You're Sandy? Man, dude, I was waiting for you on the strip in Colombia, but you didn't show!" "No fucking way!" I replied. Now this was crazy; I mean how small had this smuggling world become?

I had been working side by side with this guy named Bosco for the past eight months, and come to find out, his best friend had been Vicente from the hotel room in Panama! Could it get any crazier? We continued to discuss what happened to me and then what had happened to him. With the failure of the deal and my capture in Panama, he had been solicited to bring a freighter full of weed from Colombia to California. Apparently, it had been a rickety old freighter and had broken down somewhere along the coast of California. After floating close to a month off the coast and nearly starving to death, he claimed it had almost been a welcome relief once the Coast Guard and DEA boarded the freighter and arrested them, and it probably saved his life. He told me he nearly cut off one of his fingers to use as bait, he was so hungry.

After lengthy discussions with Bosco, during which he confided in me about his past, I learned there had been a mob affiliation with the boys that had put that Colombian trip together, just as I had hypothesized. Vicente had been Italian as well as Bosco, and with the Jewish New York attorney…well, as the saying goes, "if it walks like a duck…" Nonetheless, Bosco and I became good friends and spent many hours together on the tennis courts and hosting guacamole parties. (A guacamole party was a big event at Big Spring in lieu of anything more exciting.)

Bosco was like most of the smuggler crowd, in his mid- to late-thirties with a middle-class upbringing in "white-bread" Dallas, Texas. This common thread went throughout the smuggling community. At least, the ones I knew. Unfortunately, they all now resided with me here in Big Spring. It was a small slice in time when we were some of the most influential drug smugglers of the era. My father had once said to me, "If you fly with the crows, you're a crow." Was I running with the wrong crowd? I never really thought so, although as I sat in prison, I began to wonder.

There were also inmates of some notoriety. Gregg Lott was a University of Texas quarterback whose girlfriend was Farah Fawcett. The compound was littered with other guys like Gregg. Another gentleman from Dallas was the Texas Doubles Tennis Champion, a real country club kind of guy. Another was the Prime Minister of Turks and Caicos. He had been convicted of drug trafficking and now resided two rooms down the hall from me. Two doors down in the opposite direction was a doctor from Tennessee, who got caught up in a drug scandal somewhere along the line. "Doc," as we called him, sent me a copy of Elvis Presley's last prescription, dated August 15th, 1977, and signed "George Nichopolous, MD." It was written for Diluadid,

Quaalude, Dexedrine, Percodan, Amytal, and Biphetamine. Elvis died from an overdose on August 16th, 1977. Crazy. I hung that prescription in a frame in my office. Big Spring was a melting pot of white, middle-class drug traffickers.

Overall, life was pretty good at Big Spring. Sunday was a day for family and friends to visit, and some even spent the whole weekend. I always found it somewhat distracting, however, because this forced me to move out of my blissful zone and into reality in which I no longer had any involvement. It was very strange and somewhat emotionally unhealthy. I found I had to embrace the situation I was in or else I would be consumed with worry. That was an interesting dynamic of the place: you had to immerse yourself into the camp life for sanity's sake, which was not necessarily a bad existence. There is an old saying; "If you can't do the time, don't do the crime." I don't think that really applied to our situation because this place was just too much like a great summer camp.

I had concluded that the government created these country club prisons because they didn't know quite what to do with us. We were the children of the middle class and that meant we were the sons of the system itself: the sons of judges, lawyers, and politicians, a part of society that represented the establishment. Drugs were so prevalent that many traffickers thought the legality of them imminent. As I said earlier, we thought we were on the frontier of a new industry. Prohibition didn't work in the 1920s and the War on Drugs wasn't working either. Historically, it has been proven not to work. Alas, the War on Drugs is an industry in itself and legalization of weed would simply bankrupt it.

In fact, we saw the War on Drugs as so ineffectual that after our release from Big Spring, we gave it the finger and planned a reunion in Port Aransas. We all flew in on our personal planes to what we deemed our "ex-con-vention." There were a lot of laughs, lots of drugs, lots of booze, and lots of plans for future conspiracies in the not so distant future. We were businessmen and it was business as usual.

CHAPTER TEN

There's a lady in a turban, and a cocaine tree
She does a dance so rhythmically
Now she's cryin' and singin' and having a time
(oh yeah)
And don't that cocaine tree look fine

... *"Sailin' Shoes" by Lowell George*

My sentence in Big Spring Federal Prison Camp was up in 1983. I was thirty-two years old and it was time to head home. I packed my bags, tennis racquet and all, and before I knew it, I was back at my house on Lake Austin (fortunately the new owners had defaulted on the mortgage). It took me a few days to decompress and catch my stride, but it was then back to business. However, there was a new component to my lakeside existence: I was now on parole. I was required to make monthly visits to my new, all-business female parole officer, Miss Tight Ass, for whom I needed proof that I was gainfully "and legally" employed.

During this period, Austin had become the new music capital of the millennium. I convinced Miss Tight Ass I was still owner and president of Undercover Records, the same job I had before my incarceration and throughout my trial. The courts and the parole administration were aware of the pitfalls within the music industry. Therefore, I had to prove to Miss Tight Ass that I had just made an error in judgment along the way; however, I was back on track to become a successful record executive in the music industry. There was substantial documentation to back up what I was saying, and there was an air of truth about all of it. I did own the record and publishing company, but what Miss Tight Ass didn't know was that it was all financed through my weed business. Things remained status quo. However, about this same time, the urinalysis was introduced and was immediately embraced by both the courts and their sister administrations, the probation and parole divisions. This was to create some big problems for me in both positions I held in the work force.

At this point, Boch was coming to the States for long periods of time and would stay with me while one weed deal or another unfolded. In the meantime, we were both trying to do something collaborative, apart from our smuggling. I produced an album through Undercover Records, so I would have additional props that reflected my productivity in the record industry. Boch did all the cover art. I made sure my parole officer was privy to all of it.

The band was called Extreme Heat, a white funk group, similar in sound to Earth, Wind & Fire. The band members were incredibly professional and competent. Bruce Spellman and Phil Richardson sang lead vocals. They both had rich, seasoned voices and together had incredible harmony. Neil Pederson, the keyboardist, had three scholarships and a degree from the University of Texas in classical piano. The drummer was a graduate of the Berkley School of Music. Mike Barnes, the lead guitar player, had played with Eric Clapton and many others, more than I can name. Prestigious accolades were woven throughout the entire band. As a result, every recording studio in Austin was anxious to have the opportunity to work with us, but of course my money was alluring as well.

The band and I had worked hard to put that album together. I shared an office with a friend, Tommy Joe, who also had a publishing company, Texas Crude. He worked in the genre of country while my complete focus was on Extreme Heat. Through some of Tommy's connections, he arranged for Polygram Records to come to Austin and sample the album I had recently cut. The band and I were quite proud of our accomplishment and ready to promote it. The Polygram representative showed up at my house in a black stretch limo ready to take me to various recording studios. Yeah baby, I was digging that. We rode around in that limo all day, from studio to studio, drinking champagne and discussing the future of Extreme Heat with this record executive. The recording studios were impressive; very high-tech with 48-track boards covered in lights, dials, and gauges, all pulsing with the beat of the music. It was like stepping into a spaceship. Motherfucker, it was a wild afternoon.

The limo dropped me back off at my home in the early evening and I climbed up to my small upstairs apartment, excited but spent. To my surprise, a barely legal young girl I knew was waiting in my bed naked. I threw myself down on the bed exhausted and with my hands behind my head, considered the wonder of the day's events, while this girl performed her magic. Goddamn, I thought I had it all and was absolutely sure I had made it to the big time. I guess I was just optimistic, however, as I never heard from Polygram Records again.

Nevertheless, with Boch's help, I had record jackets printed for our album in Mexico City and was even allowed to travel to Mexico to retrieve them, all with the consent of the parole administration. I flew from Austin to Dallas to catch my flight to Mexico City. Once arriving in Dallas, I learned that the flight to Mexico was delayed. I was standing in the ticket line and conversing with the girl in front of me, who turned out to be an elementary school teacher. We had been in line an hour when we learned there would be an additional six-hour delay ahead of us. We were both fairly distraught about this situation, and she suggested, "Hey, since we're stuck here so long, why don't we share a hotel room, so we'll be more comfortable?" She laughed and added, "I'm not suggesting anything sexual. This isn't about sex. That's not going to happen. I'm just thinking we could watch a movie or something and the time would go faster." Man, I wasn't looking to have sex either. However, I thought it was a great idea to get a room, knowing we had a six-hour delay, and we could share the expense. I was cool with that. Let's go!

We rented a room at the Airport Marriott and proceeded upstairs with our carry-on luggage. We entered the room, and I went directly to my bed and spread out, ready to watch a movie. She went into the bathroom upon entry. Well, goddamnit if she didn't exit the bathroom in bra and panties and jump into my bed. The rest is history—and motherfucker, I've had a hankering for elementary school teachers ever since.

On my return trip from Mexico, for some odd reason, the airline required me to purchase a first-class ticket for the few thousand album covers I was carrying, refusing to ship them as cargo. Therefore, we rode back together in style, side by side;

boxes seat-belted and stacked to the ceiling. That was some funny shit!

Boch and I later traveled to New York City in order to push the record album to major labels. I met with probably eight different companies, including Warner Brothers and Capital, but no one seemed to be impressed. Fuck, it was back to the drawing board for me. While there, Boch visited *The New York Times* with his portfolio of artwork. Subsequently, they offered him the opportunity to submit two sketches, which were both published in the editorial section of the paper two separate times within the same month. This was a prestigious and unheard of event for most artists, who were generally restricted to one published print per year in the *Times*. However, even as accomplished an artist as he was, our smuggling took precedence. The excitement and the money were too compelling.

One Saturday night around three in the morning, the band and I were returning from a gig in San Antonio. We pulled up to a Taco Cabana restaurant on our way out of town. There was a policeman in the street directing traffic for the restaurant's take-out line. It was mayhem, and it was three fucking a.m. I paused for a moment and surveyed my surroundings. I was riding in a decrepit old band van with my aging band members sprawled around me. Words my sister had said to me earlier were resonating in my head, "When are you going to stop beating a dead horse?" I said to myself, "I quit." She hadn't a clue of the time and money I had wasted. I had spent four years in this endeavor and more money than I wanted to admit, without a dime of return on my investment. I had lost hundreds of thousands of dollars. The chicks, drugs, and fame that went along with the record industry were alluring for me. However, I realized it was time to move on. I thought to myself, "I'm going to open a Mexican food restaurant!"

By 1985, when I was about thirty-three, I had moved to South Austin and bought a house on Sandringham Drive in Travis Heights. Motherfucker, the party never ever stopped at this place. I still had the band and we were recording in studio sessions. However, since deciding to move on, I was gradually pulling my focus. The weed business was still booming and the late night coke sessions as well. I had various chicks living at my house, even while dating others. Life, again, was treating me well.

I had a friend and neighbor in Austin named Jeremy, who I could call if things were slow, and I found myself at four in the morning with no one to party with, since there was way too much cocaine to ever do by myself. So, I would call Jeremy, "Dude, are you up?" He was always up. He would head over to my house, and we would proceed to stay up even later, only together. It was a dark existence, however unrecognizable to us at the time. We thought we were having fun! One time, after we had been doing coke for weeks ongoing, we bet each other $100,000 that we could quit. Two days later, Jeremy discovered I had been partying with some chicks and had again ravaged myself with cocaine. He thought he was $100,000 richer. He was mistaken; I doubled down on our bet. That's right, double or nothing. He fucked up a few days later and we were then even. Crazy!

Another way to avoid doing so much cocaine was to go fishing. It kept me away from party central and helped me focus on something else. During these South Austin years, I would grab my latest squeeze, maybe a few friends, and head on down to Port Aransas, "a drinking village with a fishing problem." I took multiple off-shore fishing trips in a chartered fifty-foot yacht, complete with an air-conditioned salon, tuna tower, and outriggers. I loved that shit! With beautiful girls onboard and a big badass fishing boat, I felt pretty damn important.

At some point, my mother informed me that she had bought a new twenty-one-foot ski boat and was storing it in Rockport where our family had a condo. Rockport is a quaint little town, thirty minutes north of Port Aransas, located on Copano Bay, which has access to the Gulf. Well, motherfucker, I decided I would take her new little boat offshore. I just knew I would be a skilled captain given all the offshore charters I had taken.

One weekend, I suggested to Jeremy, "Dude, let's go fishing!" He never knew what peril he would be in by accepting my invitation. We drove down to Rockport, hooked the boat and trailer to my truck, then drove to Port Aransas and offshore we went—insanely, without checking the weather ahead of time, without a radio, without a skilled captain, and, most ridiculously, in a ski boat. I did, however, have all the latest fishing equipment, including rods and reels any dumbass would ever need.

This was sometime in early December 1985. The weather was still accommodating and actually quite pleasant. We headed offshore at sunrise on a beautiful and smooth sea, approximately sixty miles out. We ended up having a killer day, catching sailfish, tuna, and mahi mahi. We were having a blast.

About four in the afternoon, we decided we'd had enough and it was time to head back. However, the weather was starting to turn, with rough seas and gusty winds, so we thought it best to stop and wait it out, maybe even smoke a joint and drink a beer or two. No doubt, there was a completely clueless captain in charge of decisions.

Oh, my god, the seas began to get worse, becoming more and more treacherous while we floated idly along, smoking our joint and sipping our beer. The winds had picked up as well and were beginning to howl. Darkness was starting to envelope us. Little did we know, a fierce "norther" was approaching. Eventually, I realized we needed to fire up the boat and head in. However, we were sixty something miles offshore when I came to this realization. It was time to get the fuck out of there! Oh, man, the seas were beginning to crash over the bow of the boat as we struggled just to keep her afloat. It was becoming terrifying.

It was dark as we headed in, with zero lights on the horizon to help with my navigation. The waves were incredibly high from trough to crest, taking three boat lengths to reach the top. We inched up each one, foot by foot, praying we wouldn't flip over backward and capsize. Then we had to power perpendicular down the backside and ready ourselves for the next one. With every wave we were fucking sure we were dead! After two hours of this ongoing nightmare of high screaming winds and roller-coaster waves continuously crashing over the bow of the boat, blinding us with salt spray and knocking us about, I looked over at Jeremy with knees knocking uncontrollably and said two words: "life jackets?" Jeremy slowly looked over at me and said "yes." He was the calmest motherfucker I'd ever seen, despite his sheer terror. Apparently, he had a lot of misplaced confidence in his captain.

I suggested to Jeremy he might want to take a moment to go below and get the jackets while I tried to maintain command of this motherfucker. My fingers were numb from gripping the wheel with such force and my muscles extremely tense from trying to hold it steady. We struggled to get the jackets around our necks and the straps wrapped around our waists as the boat bucked and rocked like a rodeo bull. I must say we both looked pretty silly with these small, bright-orange life jackets around our necks, almost as if we were swimming in some public pool with the rest of the children on summer vacation. But at least we felt a little safer…well, not really. When you have to put a life jacket on, things are not necessarily going very well.

I was thirty-four and had never been this terrified in my entire existence, no exaggeration. There was little said between us as we anxiously kept our focus on the horizon, scanning for any semblance of lights from shore. However, it was nearly impossible to see, as waves relentlessly crashed over us every few seconds, blinding us with salt spray that we desperately tried to wipe away. It would be six hours before we saw the slightest twinkle. We were screwed!

About ten at night, we finally spotted lights on the horizon. At such a distance, I couldn't differentiate between Port Aransas, Rockport, and Corpus Christi. We were still hours from shore. Port Aransas was the only entry for any of these three locations. Boats, large seagoing vessels, and barges all needed to enter the jetties of Port Aransas to get to any of these ports. If I chose the wrong lights, we would be in serious trouble.

I was so nervous trying to calculate which was which, I mistakenly chose the lights of Corpus Christi, the most iridescent of the three. Bad choice. After two additional hours, we found ourselves a mile off shore from Corpus Christi beaches. We could even see headlights running parallel to the coastline. I knew we were screwed. I asked Jeremy to hand me the flare gun, and we shot off about three rounds. We were in bad trouble, and the fuel gauge was reading empty. We were fucking scared. However, I could not imagine beaching someone else's new boat. I turned to Jeremy and said, "Dude, I can't beach this fucking boat. It's not mine."

I had quite a conflict going on in my head: save our lives or save the boat. I thought I could do both. I saw a working oil rig a few miles behind us and decided we would go there and tie up to wait out the storm. Hell, we had made it this far, and it was not in my nature to ruin other people's stuff, even in life-and-death circumstances. I was fairly accomplished at surviving,

I was almost sure. "Game on, motherfucker," I tearfully said to myself.

So, incredibly, Jeremy and I headed back offshore. He never said a word. Anyone in his right mind would've beached that motherfucker without a second thought, but there we went. We slowly maneuvered the boat back toward the rig, battling the waves, wind, and salt spray all over again. After another forty-five minutes, we eventually arrived at the rig. My plan was to throw the anchor around one of the rig's stabilizing pipes to secure the boat. By my directive, Jeremy scrambled to the bow with the anchor in one hand, holding on to the railing for dear life with the other, the entire time bracing against the waves crashing over the top of him. He could have been washed overboard easily. Both of us were still completely terrified, but hopeful as we approached the rig. It was close to midnight by this time.

It took numerous attempts to get secured. We would motor up, trying to get close enough to throw the heavy anchor, yet maintain a safe distance from the rig. I would propel the boat forward, but the seas kept shooting us backward every few seconds with each wave. Each time I got close, Jeremy would throw the anchor and line toward the pipes, but it always seemed to fall splashing into the sea. With each throw he became more exhausted and discouraged. It was a slow, frustrating process.

Finally, the anchor caught on the pipe, and we were hooked to the rig. I ran forward to help Jeremy let out enough anchor line to keep us from smashing up against the steel pipes. We were now attached and bobbing like a forgotten cork. Incredible! We had spent the last nine hours trying to survive and had now been on the water for a total of nineteen hours. We were exhausted. Our eyes looked like they were bleeding, they were so red from the salt spray and crashing waves we had battled to get this far. We were both incredibly relieved to be safely secured to the rig, and sat there in the boat, wet, stupefied, and exhausted. We looked at each other in disbelief and I said, "Damn, dude." He replied, "Unreal," and stared back at me in wonderment. So there we were, seesawing out in the ocean in the dark at one o'clock in the morning. We were cautious about any feelings of accomplishment. Who knew if this line would hold? We would soon find out.

Suddenly, a worker appeared one hundred feet above us on the rig. We couldn't tell if he was taking a piss or smoking a cigarette. He apparently saw us because a short time later, we heard the deep "woosh woosh woosh" of a helicopter approaching in the night. It was the Coast Guard! For the first time in my life, I was elated to see the cops. It landed on the helipad of the rig and four Coast Guard personnel exited and came to the railing.

There we were tied to the rig far below in the middle of the night, smoking a cigarette. Incredibly, the captain of the helicopter was female! She approached the railing dressed in full uniform, including flight helmet, and shouted down to us with her bullhorn, "What seems to be the nature of your distress?" Are you fucking kidding me? Jeremy and I looked at each other in complete amazement. With my hands cupped around my mouth, I shouted back, "A couple of assholes lost!" I mean really, "What is the nature of your distress?" She had to be kidding—with the wind howling at forty miles an hour and the seas crashing over the top of us in the middle of the night, let alone tied to a fucking rig in the middle of the ocean? Was she crazy? I knew I was, but a Coast Guard captain who had just piloted her aircraft in the same motherfucking storm didn't seem to recognize the severity of our desperation? What kind of question was that? I still couldn't believe my ears.

Through her bullhorn, she then shouted, "Would you like to come aboard?" "Well, hell fucking yes, we'd like to come aboard," I thought to myself, then replied, "Well, hell fucking yes!" again with my hands cuffed around my mouth. She next bullhorned us back, "Stand by and we will throw a rope ladder down to you." We looked at each other in complete bewilderment. This would be interesting. After a few minutes, a one-hundred-foot rope ladder came thundering down over the side of the rig. The captain then shouted, "Come aboard, sailors." Huh? "How the hell are we going to get that accomplished?" we both pondered incredulously.

The boat was attached to the rig; however, we were about fifty feet away from the now dangling rope ladder. The force of the waves was too strong for only one of us to pull the boat forward using the attached anchor line. It would take the two of us together. The problem was that if we both got the boat to the rope ladder, and then one jumped on, the one left behind would not be strong enough to pull it back to the ladder alone. Together, we would have to pull the boat up, and together, like Siamese twins, leap onto the rope ladder in unison.

This was some scary shit at one o'clock in the morning, in high seas, and as exhausted as we were, but the decision was made. We moved to the bow and desperately struggled with the rope to get the boat up and under the ladder. After a "one, two, three," we then both leaped on each side of the ladder, as the boat rocketed out from under us. We were left swinging on the flimsy ladder in the middle of the night with only the ferocious seas beneath us. It was terrifying! The rope ladder was wet, the seas were smashing against us, the wind was howling, and all the while the ladder was twisting and turning…twisting and turning. There we were dangling in the dark, together in the worst dance imaginable.

Jeremy labored up the ladder ahead of me, one rung at a time. I followed shortly behind him. It was right hand, left foot, left hand, right foot, over and over, one at a time, up the slippery rungs, afraid to look down. When we arrived at the platform, the crew pulled us over the railing, first Jeremy and then me. We stood frozen in fear on the metal grilled walkway among about ten jaw-dropped crewmembers and four uniformed and helmeted Coast Guard with that big-ass chopper positioned on the helipad above.

The Coast Guard captain, still helmeted but, noticeably, a good-looking blonde chick, asked us, "Are you OK?" We, in turn, replied, "Fuck if we know!" Other dialogue was exchanged between us then the lovely captain asked, "Would you guys like to be flown into Corpus and taken to a hotel? You'll have to pay your own way, though. Do you have any money?" Well, there we stood shirtless and in our swimsuits, realizing that we didn't have our wallets. "No, our wallets are still on the boat," I said, pointing down a hundred feet to the black water below. "Do you want to retrieve them?" she inquired, as if it would be some fucking cakewalk. No, we would not be returning, at least not tonight, thank you. Hell no, we weren't going back to that boat, was she crazy? "What's our next option?" I asked pleasantly. "Any thoughts about me coming home with you?" I almost asked, then shook my head in disbelief at my impulses even in such dire circumstances.

"Well," she replied, "your other option is to spend the night here on the rig and make a fresh start, come morning." We were rather bewildered, but decided we had no choice but to stay. The rig crew chief then welcomed us aboard and extended his hospitality. Afterwards, the hot blonde captain excused herself, and she and her crew jumped back in their chopper and sped off into the distance. I'll miss her.

I had never been on a working rig before, but this baby was nice. It was like a hotel on top. They escorted us inside, and first took us to their cafeteria where they proceeded to feed us hot dogs, hamburgers, French fries, and drinks. It was goddamned fabulous inside this place—I couldn't believe it. Jeremy and I had yet to say two words to each other. We just shook our heads in indescribable amazement. We were actually safe and alive. We were also being fed and comforted by roughnecks who were as kind and welcoming as the staff of any five-star hotel. Fucking crazy! Who would have believed it?

One may think this would be the end of it, but far from it. They took us to separate sleeping quarters, gave us some dry clothes, and put us to bed. However, around three in the morning, one of the crew members woke me up to inform me that my boat had broken loose and drifted away. I got up and followed him outside. No boat. "Fuck," I thought to myself, but what could I do? I thanked him for his concern and retreated back to my sleeping quarters and slumber.

Morning came and they woke us, again, to let us know there would be a crew ship arriving shortly that would take us back to port. Man, was I feeling like a dumbass or what. Actually, both a dumbass *and* a what! First, they offered us breakfast and tried to console me as well as they could. I was very appreciative of their concern, but fuck, "what a goddamned idiot," I thought to myself. Soon the crew boat arrived, and Jeremy and I were boarded for our sullen ride back to port, boatless, yet alive—although I remained unconvinced that was acceptable.

Once I got on board I went straight to the wheelhouse and introduced myself to the captain. He was already aware of our situation; in fact, everybody that worked in the Gulf seemed to be aware of our situation. From my understanding, we were the butt of many jokes throughout the entire Gulf of Mexico, or so I suspected. I gave a rundown to the captain of our predicament and asked him if he would take a moment and use his radar to look for my boat. "Yeah, man," he warmly agreed.

After we pulled away from the rig, we started to scan the horizon for my mother's boat, "my mother's" being the operative words. Well, there it was, floating about a mile and a half away, just like a message in a bottle. I could not believe our luck. We motored toward it and pulled alongside—fucking incredible. I dove into the water ten feet below and swam over. I climbed on board and tried to start it. "Yang, yang, yang, yang. Yang, yang, yang, yang. Yang, yang, yang, yang," the starter turned over and over and over. The engine wouldn't fire. It was out of gas.

I suddenly appreciated the direness of our situation. I realized that once we had gotten to the rig and tied up, the motherfucker had run out of gas, completely run out of gas. One moment longer and we would have stalled, drifting without power in the tormented seas, the waves pushing us further offshore and away from any rescue. How much luckier could I have been?

The crew boat then threw me a line and towed me back into port, safe and sound. I bought them a case of beer for their efforts. That was the extent of the captain's request for all he had done. We trailered the boat and drove back to Rockport. My mother never knew. Crazy!

CHAPTER ELEVEN

*Since the beginning it hasn't changed yet
People fly high begin to lose sight
You can't see very clearly when you're in flight*

*It's high time that you found
The same people you misuse on your way up
You might meet up
On your way down…*

… "On Your Way Down" by Alan Toussaint

After the fishing trip, Boch came back to Austin to collect his portion of the cash from another successful load we had completed in Mexico. We were driving around town, when Boch turned to me and said, "Hey, let's stop by and visit a friend of mine named Rob." I said, "Sure, whatever you want to do." We had absolutely nothing going on and this was the kind of shit we did, spontaneity at its best. He gave me a bit of "heads up" about who and where he'd met his friend Rob. Apparently, Rob was also a customer of Ricardo's in Mexico and, therefore, a friend of Boch's as well. Boch informed me ahead of time that Rob was notorious for losing loads; in other words, he was a loser. However, he was engaged in the same weed-smuggling business that I was, and Ricardo was his connection. Hey, this would be a common reality at least. Off we went to meet him.

Arriving at Rob's girlfriend's house in West Austin, he greeted Boch and me at the door. "Hey, Boch, what's up?" Boch replied, "Not much, dude. I want you to meet my friend Sandy." Rob and I exchanged salutations. He appeared fairly normal. We sat around and chatted a while, the conversation full of consummate bullshit and nothing of importance. We talked a little about Ricardo and how crazy it was that we both bought weed from him, blah, blah, blah. Boch eventually asked Rob, "So what's going on?" and Rob replied, "I lost another one." Well, hell, here Boch and I had just completed another successful load, and Rob was on the down-and-out. We both had nothing but empathy for him. "Dude, we're sick to hear that," Boch and I expressed in unison. We offered a number of lame platitudes to try and cheer him up as we were making our departure. We said our good-byes and hopped into my pickup and headed toward the house. As Boch had indicated, "Rob is notorious for losing loads." I didn't give him a second thought. It was quite awhile before I ran into Rob again.

The weed business was booming for me, and the nightlife as well. It was not unusual for me to party all night and sleep most of the day. As owner of Undercover Records, well shit, it went with the territory. I hated cocaine, but chicks loved it, and I loved chicks. For a guy that hated cocaine, I sure did snort my fair share. I have to admit, it was ridiculous. Maybe I was a chick addict, I don't know. I was never quite sure why I abused coke so much. It never computed.

Nevertheless, I was out one night and a friend of a friend told me about some other yahoo that sold it. I called him up and was on my way, simple as that. I arrived at his trailer, just off the corner of Oltorf and Lamar, for a little additional "late night abuse" sometime after midnight, and knocked on his door. "Dude, I need a couple of grams—can you help a brother out?" Of course he could; that's what he did. He invited me into his crack house trailer and proceeded to dole out a couple of grams for me, nothing out of the ordinary. Then who walked out from the rear bedroom—none other than Rob Lickmacock! I was shocked and in disbelief.

"Rob, you motherfucker, what the fuck is going on?" I said, completely surprised to see him "Nothing dude, just trying to get back on my feet," he explained. "Dude, this is crazy, I can't believe I am running into you. Is everything OK with you?" I said in my party-induced rhetoric. "Yeah, man, this is what's going on with me." "Right on brother, great to see you!" Back and forth we conversed with the regular bullshit exchanges. Wow, to see Rob like this, even more down-and-out than before, pitiful and confused. I said to him, "*Vato*, I've got more weed than I know what to do with. Can you help me unload a bit of it?" He perked up and responded, "I'll do what I can. I think I've got the right guys that can help." Eventually, I left the trailer after purchasing my two grams of whiff and exchanging numbers with Rob.

As it turned out, Rob, to his credit, did know just the right guys. They were cash buyers with plenty of expendable funds. These guys could rock! Motherfucker, it was now off to the races! Rob had become my newest best friend. We were selling a thousand pounds at a time, and the revenue was incredible. We were banking it! At some point during the next few months,

I approached Rob and said, "We have got to do something responsible with this cash, rather than waste it away on more chicks and more blow!" He couldn't have agreed more. He had seen the dark side and never wanted to return.

Later, I discovered Rob was actually a pretty good cook. This was completely foreign to me (although I could make a mean salad for four hundred), and I thought he could possibly be a great addition for my planned Mexican food restaurant. We were partners in the weed sales, so why not partner up in the restaurant business? I informed Rob of my idea for a taco bar. I thought this was a pretty good choice for turning our newfound cash into something legitimate. He didn't have any other ideas, so my restaurant concept became our focus.

After my time in Cholula, I knew exactly what our formula should be. I had frequented a taco bar in Cholula for many years and had fallen in love with the food. I had eaten in this place more times than I wanted to admit, but the food was terrific. The grill was out front in the seating area, so customers could watch their tacos being prepared. The food they made was over the top. I knew if this concept were brought to the States, it would be a slam dunk, so I presented it to Rob. He got behind it, and we had a plan.

We subsequently drove around Austin looking for locations between our weed sales. My god, we drove around and around. At some point during one of these long and extended rides in Rob's black, early-model Continental, I turned to him and said, "Dude, we have got to stop driving around. I'm starting to get carsick, motherfucker. Let's make our stand and jump in with both feet, goddammit! We need to commit." Though we both had our reservations, it was time to make a move, and he reluctantly agreed. We found a location, an abandoned 7-11 in South Austin that had been vacant for years. It was perfect, right around the corner from my new house and right down the street from his rental. It couldn't be any more convenient. Our taco bar was on the fast track.

Rob and I retreated to my house, along with Boch, to throw back a few drinks and any additional illicit substances we had. Again, it was business as usual. The questions to be considered were, "What are we going to name the taco bar?" and "How are we going to design the inside?" After brainstorming for a few inebriated hours, we finally came up with the name "Guera's." Boch had been instrumental in our selection, and we were all awash with exuberance. *Guera* meant "white bitch" in Spanish. The inside design was left to me because I was trying to duplicate the taco bar in Cholula. Everyone was comfortable with both solutions. Boch then came up with the font we would use for signage, and Guera's was born! It was early 1986.

We hired our great and mutual friend George to do the build-out. He did an incredible job! The place was unfolding better than expected. George, another friend Jaime, and I laid the Mexican tile for the bar and had a great time doing so. With the completion of every aspect, we were all very proud. George and his crew were craftsmen, and at the end of each day this was reflected in their work. Rob would make an occasional visit, whenever required, but he was busy planning his marriage to his new girlfriend, Kathi, and we were all happy to give him the time. Boch designed the exterior piling sign, along with the large "Guera's" insignia that graced the bright pink awnings, installed to produce shade for our outside diners. Baby, once again, we were on fire!

My house was less than a block away and already headquarters for our weed business, but now it became HQ for our restaurant as well. I had an "interview" couch where I lured many an unsuspecting waitress to undergo the application process. I thought a job at Guera's could be the job of a lifetime, and as a legend in my own mind, I was sure I could convince them of the same. HQ was party central for us as well as the rest of our ne'er-do-well friends that clung to us like glue. The cocaine and whiskey were flowing and the weed sales as well. How do you stop that? Apparently, I couldn't.

As good as life was for all of us, things were beginning to unravel for me. It simply became too much. Boch lived with me, Rob was always there snorting his coke, and then there was the party, the party that never ended. Unfortunately, I was still on parole. In clinical terms, I was firmly planted in the "double bind." The cocaine use was relentless and the piss tests as well. I could hardly spend any more time in the sauna trying to sweat the shit out of my system. I was a mess and out of control. Under normal circumstances I would've stopped. That would have been the most prudent solution, but I was a goddamned drug dealer with the entourage that went with it. It was crazy!

There were many times Miss Tight Ass would come by for one of her home visits, and there would be no less than a thousand pounds of weed in my garage. Again, it was fucked up! The urinalysis was about to take me down. Ironically, sex, drugs and rock 'n' roll, my closest friends for years, were becoming my worst enemies. I was devastated over our breakup. I was not making any excuses, and I took full responsibility for my behavior, but the external forces (i.e., Rob and Boch) were not making things any easier for me. I had to tell Boch at one point, "You have got to go. I can't continue like this. The party has got to stop!" Unfortunately, I had come up with this particular solution a tad late. Boch grew resentful—talk about a "double bind," Jesus! My best friend, put out with me for my attempted departure from the party; just one word: crazy!

One afternoon, Rob gave me a ride downtown for my monthly visit with Miss Tight Ass, nothing out of the ordinary; only today the ordinary was about to change. I never came back home. They revoked my parole, arrested me on the spot, and Big Spring Prison Camp, here I come again, all in the name of dirty piss tests. The saunas apparently had not been working as well as I had hoped. I spent another twelve months at that sports complex. The whole time, Rob and I stayed in contact, and I sent my share of any monies that were needed to keep the restaurant going. He was my bud, my partner in crime, and my new partner in the restaurant. It was our code of ethics; it was our hippie mantra: take care of your brother, especially under duress. I just knew Rob would look out for our best interests.

Big Spring was the same frolicking time as before, and my tennis game got even better. A good friend, Roy, took care of my house while I was gone. He kept the lawn mowed and the plants watered, and completed any other additional chores required. He also kept the A/C on low to prevent any mildew or decay on the inside.

Fast-forward to my release in the fall of 1987. Once I arrived home, the house was in immaculate order and all my things in their place, just as I had left them. One of my girlfriends met me at the door in a revealing outfit that she immediately discarded. It was as if I had never left. Boch and Rob showed up later that afternoon to share in what I thought was going to be an incredible reunion with high-fiving and hugging, lots of laughs, and maybe a whiskey or two.

Apparently, Rob had a different agenda planned. After about five minutes of glad-handing, Rob nervously confronted me with puffed chest and said, "I am taking the restaurant and there is nothing you can do about it because it's all in my name anyway." (Actually, we had done that purposefully because I had a federal conviction and we were worried about getting a liquor license.) "Hmm…" I replied, as I stood back and tried to assess this brazen remark. It was obvious to me that Rob had spent hours in front of the bathroom mirror practicing the words he had just delivered. I also concluded that Rob was close to puking, as he paced around the living room waiting for my response. He was anxious and unsure what my reaction might be. Could there be a fistfight about to ensue? His brow was sweaty and he looked pitiful and confused, just as I had seen him where I'd found him back at that crack house.

I began to recognize that Rob had accomplished very few successes in his life before Guera's, and now that he was nearing forty, married, and scared, he felt he had few options left. Robbery must have seemed necessary. No telling what role or influence Rob's new portly wife Kathi had played in these proceedings. Apparently, she was just hungrier than most. The words that Boch had once said to me on an earlier occasion were resonating in my head, "Never partner up with Rob." Unfortunately, I didn't listen. I then looked back at Rob and said, "Well, my man, you're the one that has to live with yourself." Rob acknowledged my response and on the turn of a dime, left my house with Boch in tow. I'm sure he couldn't have gotten out of there fast enough, his "coup de thievery" complete.

And that is the story of Guera's. One might think that would be a sad ending for yours truly, but not the case. Rob, in his defense, eventually moved the restaurant to a new location where it has become one of the most iconic and popular restaurants in Austin. What he doesn't know is that every time I pass the new Guera's sign, the same exuberance washes over me, and rewardingly, he pays homage to me. So, if you are ever in the mood for a delicious taco and you're rolling down Congress Avenue; please stop by Guera's and tell Rob "hi" for me. He will always require compassion—most posers do.

EPILOGUE

I've did my time in that rodeo
It's been so long and I've got nothing to show
Well I'm so plain loco
Fool that I am I'd do it all over again

... "Mercenary Territory" by Lowell George

With things at a close in Austin, it was time to saddle up and ride toward a new horizon. I decided Houston, Texas, was the next stop along my way. Coincidentally, my good friend and builder, George, had also moved to Houston around the same time. We had a long and fruitful relationship throughout the years we spent together. George had moved his construction company and crew to Houston while I had stumbled into the new and booming cell phone industry. I built that business into a six-store retail chain, and George did the build-out for all of the stores. Things were "going on" yet again.

The cell phone stores rewarded me handsomely, and during this period, George built a million-dollar mansion for me outside of Houston on Clear Lake. Life was good. George took the plans he had drawn for my house and duplicated the same structure, only on steroids, on his ranch outside of Bandera. It was a beautiful place for a beautiful guy.

As the years went by, I eventually sold all of the stores and retired from the telecommunications industry. Along my journey, I discovered that the corporate world I was so enamored with was actually more corrupt than the drug business I struggled so hard to quit. I had never seen so much corruption and couldn't wait to get away. I gave up the Ferragamo shoes and Hermes ties and even my 500 SL Mercedes for a return to my faded blue jeans and a truck. The smuggling business had been way more honorable and a hell of a lot more fun, but that was then and this is now. My background mandated that I use everything I had learned in first grade: your handshake is true; you live by honor and honor alone; you treat everyone as your brother; and you never take advantage of the more unfortunate. The corporate world had tested my resolve and it was time to go.

Some people may think I am simply rationalizing my self-serving smuggling lifestyle and my previous illegal behavior, but I never defined it as anything less than honorable. It was for the Cause and solely against the Man. I was just sure "they" were wrong and I was right. King of my own universe? Perhaps, but in my mind I was never a fraud, only an outlaw.

Would I want my children to follow in my footsteps? Of course not. It's much too dangerous today, and it's yesterday's news. However, what I learned along the way about life and "the big picture," I openly share with anyone, especially my children. I try to offer love as my father did. I tell them frequently, "Use me. I can be a flashlight in the dark for you." My oldest son once said to me, "Dad, you're the smartest guy I know." I only wish I would have said that to mine. Even with my multiple times in multiple prisons, I have never been ashamed of any past behavior. It was way too much fun, and what a great run it was!

After my departure from the telecommunications industry, I headed to West Texas to "drill me an oil well." While flying my plane into the proverbial setting sun, it just so happened that I unintentionally found myself passing over Big Spring Federal Prison Camp. Crazy. I looked outside my window, and focusing on the memories below, gently tipped my wing, then my hat, and murmured softly to myself, "*Adios*, motherfuckers!"

...and then I went to Africa.

H. R. STOKES III

Though now sixty years old, H.R. "Sandy" Stokes still tries to maintain his arrogant, renegade, womanizing, outlaw status. He still drinks in excess, chews tobacco, and spews a lot of bullshit. He vacillates between Port Aransas, Texas, and the African continent, leaving his libidinous moll, two redheaded sons, and a couple of dogs behind. This is his first in a series of memoirs.

Made in the USA
Columbia, SC
02 December 2021